Learning Resource Centre

THOMAS ROTHERHAM COLLEGE

A tradition of achievement · A future of opportunity

.			

VULCAN

VULCAN
last
of the
V bombers

DUNCAN CUBITT with **KEN ELLIS**

CHANCELLOR
PRESS

About the authors

Duncan Cubitt is a (semi-retired) photographer, well known for his in-depth bowls coaching books, the most famous being *Bowl with Bryant*, published in 1983. Duncan was in the Life Boys (1960-1961) but has now left the sea behind for aviation interests with the magazines *Airforces Monthly* and *FlyPast*. He lives in Stamford, Lincolnshire, with his wife Margaret, daughters Sara and Jessica, and Barney the dog.

Ken Ellis is a retiring journalist who has specialised in writing about retired aircraft. He was was never a Life Boy, but has been a Scouser once or maybe twice. He edits *FlyPast* and avoids daylight. He lives in the People's Republic of Rutland with his wife Pam, has a cat named Fleas and a fish called Wanda.

This book is dedicated to all members of the Vulcan Display Team, RAF Waddington, be they volunteer or full time, past or present, aircrew or groundcrew. They have given to the public the beauty and spectacle of a Vulcan long after we had any right to expect it, and for that we thank them all.

First published in Great Britain in 1993 by Osprey Publishing
This edition published in 1996 by Chancellor Press, an imprint of Reed Consumer Books Limited
Michelin House, 81 Fulham Road
London SW3 6RB
and Auckland, Melbourne, Singapore and Toronto

© Reed International Books Ltd/Key Publishing

ISBN 1 85152 968 3

Edited by Tony Holmes
Page design by Paul Kime
© Cutaway by Mike Badrocke/Aviagraphica
©Three-view by Dennis Punnett
Printed in China

STOP PRESS
Following questions in the House of Commons, the MoD announced on Wednesday 27 January 1993 that all attempts to keep the Vulcan XH558 within the structure of the RAF had failed. The aircraft was put up for tender in the week beginning 1 February, with a view to its disposal as soon as possible. XH558 was due for another crew check flight on the same day, and it was assumed that the aircraft would be kept in an airworthy condition for delivery to its next owner.

Above XL426 was the founder member of the Vulcan Display Team (VDT), delighting crowds after the aircraft's operational retirement during 1984 and 1985. Delivered from Woodford on 12 September 1962, XL426 was issued to No 83 Sqn at Scampton, Lincolnshire. The unit had flown Vulcan B.1s from Waddington, Lincs, from July 1957 until August 1960. To take on the B.2, they moved north to Scampton and received their first aircraft in December of that year, flying on with the type until August 1969 when the unit disbanded. From No 83 Sqn, XL426 moved to serve with the Scampton Wing, then Nos 27, 617 and 50 Sqns, finally going into the Waddington 'pool' and remaining at the base beyond the wind-down of No 44 Sqn (December 1982) and No 50 Sqn (March 1984). Beyond the disbanding of the latter unit, a cadre of Vulcan personnel remained at the station looking after, among other things, the Nimrod AEW.3 Joint Trials Unit (JTU) that was helping to evaluate the ultimately abortive home-spun UK replacement for the venerable Shackleton AEW aircraft. On a volunteer basis, they formed the VDT and picked XL426 to be their mount, the aircraft staging a few very welcome shows during the 1984 season. The number of venues increased for 1985, but this was to be XL426's last whole season. During 1986 XH558 was chosen as the successor airframe and XL426 was offered for disposal by tender

Acknowledgements

This work is essentially a history of the Vulcan through the surviving airframes and as such is largely devoted to the B.2 version. The vast majority of the photographs in the book were taken during the final weeks of display operation by Vulcan B.2 XH558. Photographs of the surviving static airframes are mostly contemporary in time with the last days of XH558. Archive material has been used where appropriate. Unless noted, all photographs are the work of Duncan Cubitt using Canon EOS 1 cameras and a range of lenses from 24 to 300 mm on Fuji RDP 135-36 and Kodak PKR 135-36 colour film; other contributors are credited with their work.

We wish to thank the following for their contributions to this book during the production stage: Dave Allport; David F Brown; Pat Chong; Alan Curry; Cliff Knox; Jane Lowndes; David Oliver; Brian Pickering/Military Aircraft Photographs; Francois Prins; Robert Rudhall; Chris Walkden and Tony Holmes at Osprey.

To the following 'Vulcan people' go our thanks for access, hospitality and resources in travelling to chronicle the survivors: Aerospace Museum, Cosford; Roger and Heather Brooks; Carlisle Airport; Castle Air Museum, Castle AFB, California; City of Norwich Aviation Museum; Delta Engineering Association; East Midlands Aeropark Visitors Centre and the Aeropark Volunteers Association; Dougie Godfrey and Harry Holmes, British Aerospace, Woodford; Imperial War Museum, Duxford; Manchester Vulcan Bomber Society; Midland Air Museum; Museum of Flight, East Fortune; Newark Air Museum; North East Aircraft Museum; Radar Moor Ltd; RAF Museum, Hendon; RAF Strike Command Public Relations; RAF Waddington; Solway Aviation Society; States of Jersey Airport; Strategic Air Command Museum, Offutt AFB, Nebraska; Stuart Stephenson; Tom Stoddart; Nigel Towler, The Cockpit Collection; Vulcan Memorial Flight Supporters' Club; Wales Aircraft Museum.

Introduction

With its unique handling characteristics, looks, sounds and smells, the Vulcan can, like few other aircraft, evoke powerful nostalgia amongst the pilots and crews who flew in them, or serviced them. With the demise of the last Vulcan squadron in 1984, I considered myself most fortunate and privileged to return to the aircraft as captain of the Display Flight for one, or possibly two seasons. This period was gradually extended by the Royal Air Force until the end of 1992 when the last remaining Vulcan's fatigue life had virtually been consumed and the hours remaining before a major service was required had all but been used up.

The aircraft is a superb pilot's machine, with enormous power but still retaining beautifully sensitive controls, even in the low speed range where all the display flying is carried out. Its near delta-shaped wing, very high stalling angle of attack and huge area of control surfaces enables it to fly in very tight turns at remarkably low speeds, all of which enhances its display appeal.

Paradoxically, the further away from operational service the Vulcan has come, the more popular it appears to be with the airshow-going public. Whilst sentiment may play a certain part in this, I believe that the Vulcan, with its all-British development and construction, is, as an awesome example of air power, second to none. As such it is part of our national heritage and I am sure that few people have not felt a surge of pride as well as exhilaration watching it power its way into a wing over or thunder around a steep turn.

It was therefore with great sadness that the crew of the Vulcan Display Flight flew their very last display at Cranfield on 20 September 1992.

Sqn Ldr Paul Millikin,
Vulcan Display Flight,
RAF Marham
January 1993

Contents

A close up of the cabin area of Vulcan B.2 XM575. Frontal glazing was minimal and the feeling of claustrophobia was mildly alleviated by two circular glazings in the jettisonable cockpit hood. During a nuclear strike, the crew would black out the entire cabin so as to avoid the chance of blindness from the weapon burst

Genesis

Below and right New Year's Day 1947 saw the issuing of a small document that was to have many ramifications. This was Specification B35/46, and it 'landed' on the desk of Roy Chadwick six days later. Chadwick was the Chief Designer for A V Roe and Company, and he had long been regarded by those who worked with him as a genius. He and his team had many successes under their belt, but it was the Lancaster bomber for which he was best known. Avro were one of seven manufacturers being invited to design and build the RAF's first-ever nuclear bomber, a four-jet aircraft intended to strike at the heart of an 'enemy', shortly to crystalise as the Soviet Union, as what became known as the 'Cold War' began to take a grip on the world. The successful contenders were to replace the Avro Lincoln (itself a developed Lancaster) and Boeing Washington. Chadwick and his team at Chadderton, Manchester, quickly rejected a 'conventional' approach to the new bomber, and Roy's mind began to centre upon a delta, initially with what much latter would be called 'end-plate' vertical flying surfaces. His first sketches and calculations still survive.

By March 1947 the delta concept was consolidated still further, and Chadwick committed this radical solution as Avro's submission to meet the Specification. Throughout this time, Chadwick was a worry to family and colleagues alike as he was clearly grossly overworked, and had been for a long, long time. He was diagnosed as suffering from shingles, yet met myriad calls upon his time and kept at the helm of the Type 698 project. Roy Chadwick turned 54 on 30 April, and seven days later Avro's response to Specification B35/46 was sent in. In late July, Sir Tom Sopwith was able to tell Chadwick in strict confidence that the Type 698 and the Handley Page HP.80 (later named Victor) had 'won' the contest on 23 July, and that prototypes were to be ordered. Wind tunnel testing at Farnborough brought about some changes in the design concept, including a single fin and rudder and a much more conventional 'nose' in which the crew were to be positioned – the shape of the Vulcan was then 'frozen'. One person, above all others, was missing the day the first-ever Type 698 took to the air. He was the man who penned its initial concept and was to interpret the RAF's needs in such a bold and satisfying manner. That man was Roy Chadwick, Avro's genius designer. He was tragically killed, in another of his designs, the Tudor

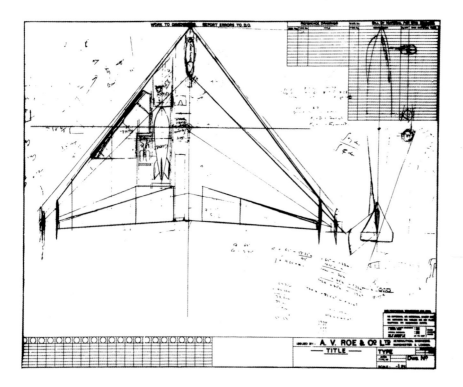

2 airliner G-AGSU, which crashed at Woodford on 23 August 1947. S D Davies, Avro's Assistant Chief Designer, miraculously escaped from the wreckage of the aircraft and went on to bring to reality the concept that his boss had pioneered. The legend would live on! (*British Aerospace Woodford*)

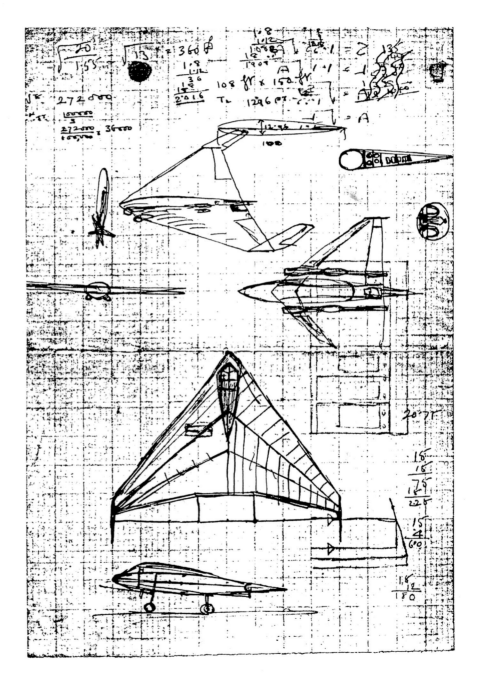

Above Wg Cdr Roly Falk eased the prototype Avro Type 698 VX770 into the air for the very first time on 30 August 1952. Officially named the Vulcan in January 1953, all involved in the project knew that they were starting something very historic. Nobody could have guessed how long that legend would keep flying, or ever have anticipated the emotion the mighty delta would engender in countless people. Problems in developing the Bristol Siddeley Olympus turbojet meant that VX770 flew with four 6500 lb st Rolls-Royce RA3 Avons. Escorted by two Avro 707s (the red 707A WD280 and the blue 707B VX790), VX770 – in all white – stunned the audiences at the SBAC display at Farnborough in September 1952. They had not seen anything like it before, but Avro's were planning to top even this act *(British Aerospace Woodford)*

Above Fitted with 9750 lb st Olympus 100 engines, the second prototype Vulcan, VX777, took to the air for the first time on 3 September 1953 – just in time for that year's Farnborough show. Here both Vulcans flew in formation with four 707s (VX790, WZ736, WZ744 and WD280). At the 1955 Farnborough, Roly Falk rolled a Vulcan with ease. The big delta was established beyond doubt as a popular performer *(British Aerospace Woodford)*

Above The huge Avro factory at Chadderton, and the assembly hall at Woodford, Stockport, set to construction of the production B.1s quickly. They were ordered in two batches; XA889 to XA913 – 25 aircraft; and XH475 to XH483, XH497 to XH506 and XH532 – 20 aircraft. XA889 made its first flight from Woodford on 4 February 1955, and was eventually fitted with the Series 101 Olympus of 11,000 lbs st that was initially intended for the type. Production aircraft were slightly longer that the prototypes, but otherwise were remarkably similar. During 1955 it was proven that buffeting could affect the strength of the outer wing sections of the delta, and modifications were made on the production line, or retrospectively, to give the outer wing area a decided 'kink', taking the aircraft away from the classic triangular look of the two prototypes. No 230 OCU at Waddington took delivery of the first service B.1s in May 1956, with No 83 Sqn bringing them into operational service in July 1957. In all, B.1s went on to serve with Nos 27, 44, 50, 83, 101 and 617 Sqns. The electronic warfare suite fitted into the rear of the more powerful and more developed B.2 was retro-fitted to some B.1s, which were redesignated as B.1As and served operationally until 1968 (*British Aerospace Woodford*)

Above The Series 201 Olympus of 16,000 lb st, plus greater electronic countermeasures located in an extended tail and many other detail refinements, gave rise to the B.2. This powerful machine was eventually to carry the Blue Steel stand-off weapon, and was schemed also to accept two of the US-built Skybolt long range stand-off weapons. The B.2 had further compound taper of the leading edge and also boasted a Rover auxiliary power unit to help it be more independent of ground facilities during times of dispersal to airfields other than V-bomber bases. By 1959 air-to-air refuelling with Valiant tankers was under trial and the B.2 was to take advantage of this range extension from entry into service. First B.2 was XH533, which made its first flight at Woodford on 19 August 1958. Deliveries to the RAF began in the 1960s. Later production aircraft were fitted with the Olympus 301 of 20,000 lbs st. Illustrated is the only flightless Vulcan – B.2 XM596 was taken off the production line in 1963 and used for a wide-ranging series of fatigue tests as the new low-level role of the Vulcan was anticipated, and data on its long term behaviour in this environment was essential *(British Aerospace Woodford)*

Above left Two Vulcan B.1s lasted as whole airframes into the 1980s. B.1 XA900 at the Aerospace Museum, Cosford, Shropshire, and Olympus test bed XA903 at the Royal Aircraft Establishment (RAE), Farnborough, Hampshire. Chronic corrosion in XA900 made it unsafe (this was an inheritance of the former static instructional airframe and not a slight on the capabilities of the museum) and it was duly scrapped in 1986. XA903 was broken up in September 1984, but the nose section lives on. Two other nose sections are preserved; B.1A XA909 at the Lincolnshire Aviation Heritage Centre, East Kirkby, and B.1 XA893 at Cosford (illustrated). XA893 served as a development airframe and was issued to the Aeroplane & Armament Experimental Establishment (A&AEE) at Boscombe Down, Wiltshire, and amongst other tasks pioneered much of the electrical fit for the up-coming B.2. It was scrapped at Boscombe, but the nose section was retained by No 71 Maintenance Unit at Bicester, Oxfordshire, and used as a travelling recruiting aid, before eventually moving on to be based at Abingdon for similar work. It was eventually collared by Cosford after

the demise of the B.1 and placed on display (Cosford is also home to Avro 707 WZ744 and Vulcan B.2 XM598)

Above B.1 XA903 was delivered to the A&AEE at Boscombe Down on 31 May 1957 and later served with the RAE at Farnborough. Among other trials it was used for Blue Steel stand-off weapon experiments, and the fitting of 27 mm cannon. The airframe was most famous for its service as an engine test-bed, and it was first used on the Concorde programme flying with an Olympus 593 under its belly. In 1973 XA903 shifted to helping another multi-national project, the Panavia Tornado, when a Turbo-Union RB.199 was fitted to its underside. It was retired in March 1979 and allocated to the fire section at Farnborough *(Military Aircraft Photographs)*

Left Scrapped in September 1984, the nose of XA903 was saved by members of the Wales Aircraft Museum and moved to their site at Cardiff-Wales Airport, Glamorgan. Here it joined XM569, delivered from Waddington the previous year

Mini-Deltas – the 707s

Below Chadwick's choice of airframe concept for the Type 698 required as much data as possible before the prototype made its first flight. One answer to this pressing need was for a series of small delta wing research aircraft to fly prior to the full-size machine, in order that the properties of the delta wing be better assessed. The very first of five 707s, all powered by Rolls-Royce Derwents, was short lived. VX784 first flew at Boscombe Down on 4 September 1949, piloted by S E Esler. After an appearance at that year's SBAC display at Farnborough, it crashed on 30 September 1949, killing Esler. The second aircraft, 707B VX790, was, like the original 707, fitted with a dorsal intake for the engine. It flew on 6 September 1950, the pilot being Roly Falk, who would be first to take the Vulcan into the air. Designed to look into the lower speed range, it was scrapped at RAE

Bedford in the late 1950s. Third aircraft was 707A WD280 (illustrated), which was the first with engine intakes in the wing roots, and therefore a layout very similar to the Vulcan itself. This aircraft first flew on 14 June 1951 and was eventually shipped to Australia for further trials. It is now privately owned in Melbourne *(British Aerospace Woodford)*

Right Assembled at Avro's facility at Bracebridge Heath, Lincolnshire, and tested from the adjacent Waddington airfield, Avro 707A WZ736 first flew on 20 February 1953, and was ordered not essentially for the Vulcan programme, but for delta research by the RAE. Retired in 1967 after auto-throttle trials, WZ736 is now on show at the Museum of Science and Industry in Manchester

Left and above A batch of four Avro 707Cs was also ordered, but in the end only WZ744 was completed, again at Bracebridge Heath, with first flight at Waddington on 1 July 1953. The 707C was a two-seat, side-by-side, trainer which the RAF envisaged would help crews transition onto the Vulcan, but in the end such a step-up was not needed. WZ744 later flew from RAE Bedford on high speed trials work and also with an early form of fly-by-wire control (in duplicated form). It is now to be found on show at Cosford

First farewell – the tankers

Below The final operational role for the Vulcan was as a tanker to help the already hard-pressed Victor K.2 fleet. This conversion of the Vulcan was always considered to be a stop-gap measure, so the resulting 'shed' housed underneath the aircraft's tail can be forgiven – it was certainly the worst-ever blemish to an exceptionally clean design. On 30 April 1982 after a request from the Ministry of Defence (MoD) in the light of the Falklands conflict then underway, British Aerospace at Woodford discussed the possibilities, and were given an immediate go-ahead, for six K.2 conversions. The first K.2, XH561, was delivered to No 50 Sqn at Waddington on 23 June, just 51 days after the go-ahead! Ignoring the speed of the conversion, the K.2 was no mean engineering feat; the hose drum unit was mounted in the former electronic countermeasures bay in the tail, with a 'shed' of wood and metal housed below it containing the drogue unit and the 'traffic light' signals array, positioned on either side, for the receiving aircraft. The copious Vulcan weapons-bay carried three plumbed-in cylindrical tanks of a similar shape to the extra-range modifications originally designed by Avro. The six K.2s were XH558, XH560, XH561, XJ825, XL445 and XM571, the latter being featured in this photo. It served with No 83 Sqn, the Scampton Wing and then No 50 Sqn, during which time it became a K.2. Eventually, the tanker was flown from Waddington to RAF North Front, Gibraltar, on 9 May 1984, where it was presented to the station and the colony. It was given the name *City of Gibraltar* and displayed at the base until it was scrapped in September 1990 *(Chris Walkden)*

Above Seen on approach to Coningsby, Lincolnshire, on 27 April 1983 is XH558 in the guise of a K.2. The white under-belly and the undersides of the trailing edges, along with the red 'tram lines', were all applied to help the receiver pilot see what he was up to against that dark wing surface. All of the K.2s were operated by No 50 Sqn. The unit had previously operated B.1s and B.1As at Waddington from August 1961 until November 1966. The first B.2s arrived in December 1965, and these, as well as the K.2s, were flown through to disbandment on 30 March 1984 – the last operational Vulcans in the RAF *(Dave Allport)*

Above On 14 March 1984, just prior to the disbandment of No 50 Sqn at Waddington, Strike Command staged a 'Farewell to the Vulcan' press day that included a Hercules full of photographers formating alongside the unit's K.2 tankers. Little did everyone realise that a similar sortie, this time with just one Vulcan, would take place eight years later and raise even more emotion! XH560 trails its hose for the benefit of the photographers. Delivered on 1 October 1960 to No 230 OCU, it joined No 12 Sqn in 1962 before another stint at the OCU, then to No 27 Sqn and finally No 50 Sqn, and conversion to K.2 tanker configuration at Woodford in 1982. After the disbandment of the unit, XH560 was ferried to Marham, Norfolk, on 29 November 1984 for destruction on the fire dump, a fate which had been realised by 1987

Right K.2 to K.2, XH560 suckles XL445 during the press sortie. After the disbandment of No 50 Sqn, XL445 was to suffer a similar fate to XH560, the Vulcan being ferried to Lyneham, Wiltshire, for fire duties on 5 April 1984, where it became instructional airframe number 8811M. Offered for tender in October 1990, the bomber's nose section was saved in September of the following year and moved to the Blyth Valley Aviation Collection at Walpole, Suffolk, to join the cockpit of B.2 XL388

Above Vulcan K.2 XH560 makes an approach 'up' the beaver tail of the press Hercules during the photo-session. From the frontal aspect, the K.2 was virtually impossible to differentiate from the B.2 variant

Left Three K.2s at rest at Waddington on 14 March 1984, just 16 days prior to the disbandment of No 50 Sqn and the end of operational flying for the Vulcan with the RAF. In the foreground is XJ825, with its hose-drum 'shed' unit clearly visible under the tail. XJ825 started life with the RAF on 27 July 1961 when it was delivered to No 27 Sqn, subsequently going on to serve with Nos IX, 12 and 35 Sqns prior to joining No 50 Sqn and being converted to tanker configuration. It never left Waddington after the disbandment of the squadron in March 1984, the Vulcan being allocated the instructional airframe number 8810M and used for battle damage repair training from February 1985. A local scrap merchant succeeded in tendering for the hulk in late 1990, and in just two hours during a fateful day in February 1991 a JCB excavator pummelled the mighty V-bomber to death. All of the K.2s have been detailed in these pages other than XH561, which was the first of the breed to be delivered. After service with the OCU , it joined No 50 Sqn, where upon retirement it was ferried to Catterick, North Yorkshire, on 14 June 1984 to become instructional airframe 8809M with the RAF's Fire Fighting and Safety School – the hulk was no longer recognisable by 1987. Thus, of the six K.2s, only XH558 is still in one piece

End of the road?

Below The bulk of the Vulcans that survived through to retirement as the operational units wound down were transferred to other squadrons and eventually assigned to new roles once grounded. The unit wind-down for the Vulcan B.2 was as follows: December 1967 No 12 Sqn; August 1969 No 83 Sqn; September 1981 No 230 OCU; December 1981 No 617 Sqn; February 1982 No 35 Sqn; March 1982 No 27 Sqn; April 1982 No IX Sqn; August 1982 No 101 Sqn; December 1982 No 44 Sqn; and March 1984 No 50 Sqn. Being large and resilient airframes, most Vulcans were ear-marked for fire dumps and rescue training work as they would take a lot of 'burns' before perishing. A sad finale for such a fine aircraft, but at least the airframes were ending their days honing the precious skills of saving life and limb. Typical was B.2 XM657 – the last Vulcan built. Delivered to the RAF in December 1964, it served with Nos 35 and 44 Sqns, and then the Waddington Wing. Flown from Lincolnshire to Manston, Kent, on 5 January 1982, the Vulcan was issued to the Air Force Department Fire Service's Central Training Establishment and was given the instructional airframe number 8734M. A pit was dug and the bomber carefully rolled forward so that the nose leg disappeared, giving the aircraft the appearance of one that had made a wheels-up landing. Training personnel to effect rescues from aircraft in unusual attitudes is an important part of training. XM657 was still performing this role early in 1993. In the foreground is a Devon C.2

Above B.2 XL392 was flown from Scamptom on 24 March 1982 and joined the fire dump at Valley, Anglesey, becoming instructional airframe number 8745M. The mighty delta still clung to life, just, during 1992. Having last flown with No 35 Sqn, it had initially served with No 83 Sqn following delivery from Woodford on 1 August 1962, moving on to service with the 'pooled' Scampton Wing before joining No 35 Sqn *(Alan Curry)*

The survivors

Thanks to a refreshing policy from the MoD in offering a comparatively large number of Vulcans for tender to private individuals and museums, and for allowing their delivery to approved airfields, more Vulcans have survived beyond retirement than has been the case with other types. No airframe is easy to preserve for a long period of time, but something of the complexity and size of the Vulcan is a very difficult proposition indeed. Ten years after most of the Vulcans joined museums or private collections, they are still with us. With the best will in the world, there will be a lot less of them about in 2003 as corrosion and changing fortunes and venues takes a hand.

The greatest attrition rate to date has been with the Vulcans allocated for 'display' at several RAF bases. For example, the V-bomber base at Finningley in South Yorkshire received B.2 XJ782 from Waddington on 4 September 1982, and it was placed on display inside the camp. The bomber was replaced as a display airframe by Meteor F.8 WL168 at a ceremony held on 10 June 1988, and XJ782 had been scrapped by October of that year. Similarly, former No 27 Sqn B.2(MRR) XH537 flew into RAF Abingdon, Oxfordshire, on 27 March 1982 and was put on display within the base. It was replaced as a display airframe by Hunter F.5 WP185 and eventually scrapped by May 1991, with the nose being preserved by Barry Parkhouse at Camberley, Surrey. During 1992, Abingdon itself closed as an RAF base.

As far as possible, all of the survivors (including XM605 at Castle Air Force Base, California) were photographed during the last months of operation of the Vulcan Display Team's XH558, making the vast majority of the aircraft illustrated contemporary in both time and state throughout the book.

A number of B.2 nose sections are extant : XH537 with Barry Parkhouse at Camberley, Surrey; XH560 with Nigel Towler's Cockpit Collection at Rayleigh, Essex; XH563 with Donald Milne at Banchory, Grampian; XL388 and XL445 with the Blyth Valley Aviation Collection at Walpole, Suffolk; and XM652 with a private owner at Burntwood, Staffs.

Left It could only be a Vulcan. The in-flight refuelling probe and the Ferranti terrain following radar 'thimble' were later modifications to the Vulcan force, the latter coming into use when the role changed from long range nuclear strike to the low-level mode. This is Newark's XM594 caught against a moody Nottinghamshire sky

XJ823 – Carlisle

Above One of a handful of Vulcans to be individually owned by a dyed-in-the-wool enthusiast, XJ823 is lovingly looked after by Tom Stoddart and his friends at the Solway Aviation Society at Carlisle Airport (or Crosby-on-Eden). Tom has worked for many years as an aircraft engineer, and was the man principally responsible for the operation, under a Permit to Fly, of Neil Moffatt's Gannet AEW.3 XL502 (G-BMYP) from Carlisle until its retirement in 1989. With his background, Tom knew that he was taking on an asset that would depreciate despite his efforts, but he stoically comments 'I just had to have one. It will have given me, and a lot of other people, much pleasure along the way'. During 1992 the Solway Aviation Society (SAS) staged a small airshow at Crosby, with the aim of starting a fund to put their collection, which includes Vampire T.11 WZ515, Canberra T.4 WE188, Lightning F.51 ZF583, Meteor NF.14 WS832 and Tom's Vulcan, into a purpose-built hangar/display hall. Now in its 32nd year, XJ823 will be able to look forward to many more years of tender loving care if SAS and Tom come up with the goods. This Vulcan was delivered from Woodford on 20 April 1961, becoming the first of its type to arrive at the newly-reformed No 27 Sqn at Scampton. With the squadron badge of an elephant, No 27 had last flown the Canberra B.2, standing down in December 1956. XJ823 was posted to No 35 Sqn in January 1963, this B.2

being the first of its type to arrive at Coningsby for the unit, which had also previously flown the Canberra B.2. From No 35 Sqn, XJ823 served with the Vulcan 'school', No 230 OCU, which was then based at Finningley. Then came service in the 'pooled' wings, respectively at Waddington and Akrotiri (in Cyprus), and then back to Waddington, where the Vulcan was reunited with No 27 Sqn again, the unit by then having moved to Waddington. After a short hop over Lincoln to Scampton and No 35 Sqn, the bomber returned to the Waddington Wing. Tom Stoddart was successful in bidding for the Vulcan by tender to the MoD, and the bomber made its last flight, to Carlisle, on 24 January 1983

Right Now in its 10th year of external display at Carlisle Airport, XJ823 is in remarkably good condition, and a fine testament to those who look after it. Uppermost on the fin is the shield of the City of Lincoln and below that the Disney cartoon character *Dumbo*, quickly utilized by No 27 Sqn as a less formal unit badge. The outfit flew Vulcan B.2s from April 1961 until March 1972 at Scampton, then reformed (this time down the A15 at Waddington) to fly the SR.2/B.2(MRR) from November 1973 until March 1982. It was reformed the following year on Tornados – the type slotted to take up the Vulcan's mantle

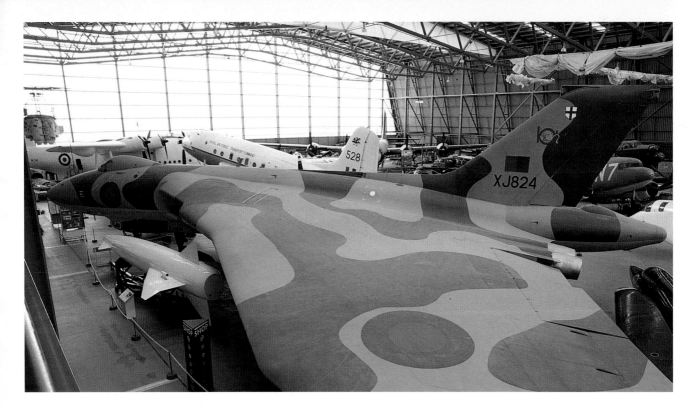

XJ824 – Duxford

Above Of the retired Vulcans, XJ824 is one of only two that can boast a roof over its head. This aircraft landed at the Imperial War Museum's (IWM) home at Duxford, in Cambridgeshire, on 13 March 1982, but had to wait almost four years for covered accommodation to materialise. The sojourn in the Cambridgeshire air was well worth it. On 9 December 1985, towed by a tractor unit 'piloted' by Roger Brooks and Heather Graves (soon to become a Brooks!), XJ824 'christened' the awesome *Superhangar* at the eastern end of the IWM complex. It needs such a space to really appreciate the shape and size of a Vulcan, and it is possible to view the delta from below and above in its new home. Displayed alongside XJ824 is an example of the Avro Blue Steel (W100) nuclear stand-off weapon, which possessed a 100-mile (185 km) range, and gave rise to the B.2 variant of the Vulcan. Powered by a Bristol Siddeley Stentor rocket engine, the Blue Steel carried a nuclear warhead of around one megaton capability, and could travel at an estimated Mach 1.6. It was an impressive size being 35 ft (10.6m) long, equipped with a rear wing which spanned 13 ft (4 m), a maximum body diameter of 4 ft 2 in (1.25 m) and an all-up weight of about 17,000 lbs (7718 kg). Not all B.2s could carry the weapon as it required bomb door

modifications as well as the installation of launch shackles. The RAF received around 60 operational Blue Steel 'rounds' from 1962, and Vulcans and Victor B.2s provided Britain's nuclear deterrent until the Royal Navy's Polaris submarines came on stream in 1967 (IWM Duxford also has a Polaris on display). Blue Steel missions continued until final phase-out in December 1970. Delivered from Woodford on 15 May 1961, XJ824 served with No 27 Sqn, the OCU and the Near East Air Force Bomb Wing (Nos IX and 35 Sqns at Akrotiri) before joining its last unit, No 101 Sqn, at Waddington, where it was earmarked for the IWM

Left The fin and rudder of the IWM's XJ824 at Duxford. Top is the shield of the City of Lincoln and below that the badge of No 101 Sqn, the last unit to operate the aircraft. The formal badge of the unit is a lion rampant and guardant upon battlements, apparent here in the more informal version 'framed' by the zero of the unit number. The squadron operated the Vulcan B.1 before taking on the B.2 at Waddington in January 1968, and eventually disbanding in August 1982. In May 1984 No 101 Sqn was reformed to operate VC10K2/3 tankers at Brize Norton in Oxfordshire

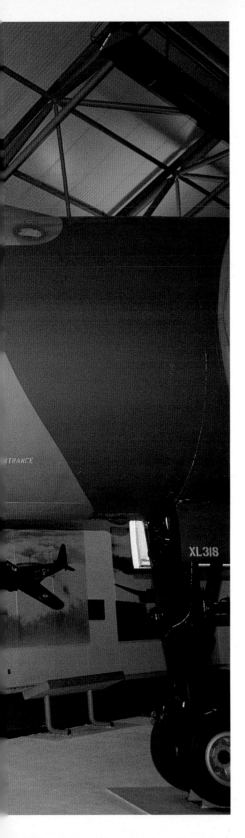

XL318

XL318 – Hendon

From 19 February to 5 March 1982 the men of the Aircraft Salvage and Repair Unit at Abingdon undertook a very different exercise, namely to dismantle and move by road Vulcan B.2 XL318 from its last operational home at Scampton to the Bomber Command Museum at Hendon, north London (now known as the Bomber Command Wing of the RAF Museum). The mighty Avro 698 was never designed to travel in such a fashion after final assembly, and this move is so far the only one such achieved – at least two potential Vulcan owners having fallen by the wayside when faced with the commercial cost of moving such an aircraft by surface transport and re-assembling it again. The feat was all the more remarkable as the aircraft had to be installed inside the museum, which was rapidly nearing completion, and thus enabling the aircraft to be built in to the structure and to meet the grand opening deadline. This means that viewing XL318 is always at close quarters, the in-flight refuelling probe being but inches from the wall! Interestingly, XL318 still carries the ARI 18288 passive electronic countermeasures/radar warning receiver fin-tip fairing, but not the Ferranti terrain-following radar 'thimble' on the nose that it wore when in service during the late 1970s. XL318 served for almost all of its life with the famous No 617 *Dambusters* Sqn, and it proudly carries their badge, which shows lightning striking a dam, on the fin. Arriving at Scampton on 1 September 1961, XL318 was No 617's first B.2, the unit having operated the B.1 until July 1961. Service with No 230 OCU followed, after which XL318 returned to No 617's fold. It fell to this airframe to undertake the squadron's last-ever Vulcan sortie on 11 December 1981, thus bringing to an end the 23-year association forged between the Avro bomber and the *Dambusters* – the Tornado GR.1 replaced the Vulcan at No 617 Sqn in January 1983. On 4 January 1982 XL318 was officially transferred to the care of the Bomber Command Museum, and was allocated the instructional airframe number 8733M

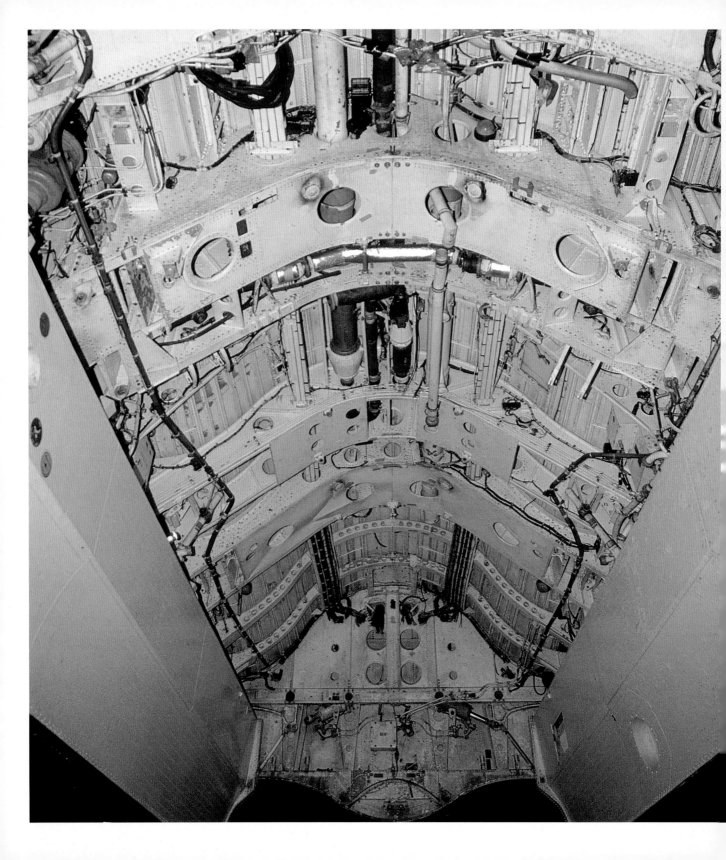

Left No matter how attractive the shape may be, this is the business end of the Vulcan. All the power and beauty was designed to allow the bomb-bay to unleash death and destruction on an enemy. The Vulcan's capacious hold could carry a wide variety of nuclear or tactical weapons including the Blue Steel stand-off bomb. Up to 21 1000 lb (454 kg) conventional high explosive bombs could be accommodated within the weapons-bay

Above A shot that is no longer possible! XL318 during the construction phase of what was then called the Bomber Command Museum during the summer of 1982. As with the Battle of Britain Museum on the same site, the construction of the building is such that the large exhibits now inside are there forever, unless structural alterations are made. The moving and re-assembly of XL318 was an astounding exercise in engineering and logistics *(Francois Prins)*

XL319 – Sunderland

When Vulcan B.2 XL319 touched down at Sunderland Airport (Usworth), Tyne & Wear, at the conclusion of its last-ever flight on 21 January 1983, it was by far and away the largest aircraft that the small airfield had ever experienced. Indeed, the RAF Jetstream T.1 that acted as crew ferry would normally have lifted eyebrows as a large movement at the airfield! The Vulcan took the runway with plenty to spare and became the centre-piece of the North East Aircraft Museum (NEAM). XL319 was delivered to the RAF on 20 October 1961, joining XL318 at Scampton with No 617 Sqn. Beyond that came use with the Scampton Wing, No 230 OCU, No 617 Sqn again, back to the OCU, No 35 Sqn and then No 44 Sqn at Waddington. It was the latter unit that undertook the offensive sorties during the Falklands campaign, but XL319 was not one of the five that went down to Ascension Island for use in the *Black Buck* missions. No 44 Sqn received its first Vulcans (B.1s) in August 1960, exchanging them for B.2s in November 1967. It disbanded in December 1982 as the last operational Vulcan *bomber* unit, with its aircraft attracting much attention by preservationists. When XL319 was flown into Sunderland Airport it was minus its in-flight refuelling probe, but has since been reunited with this bit of equipment. During the Falklands campaign, and in its aftermath, these items were like gold bricks, and even the Castle Air Force Base and Goose Bay examples had their probes removed in a global 'scrounging' operation! NEAM has established a superb collection of aircraft ranging from the fuselage of Mike Lithgow's record breaking Swift F.4 WK198, to Canberra TT.18 WJ639, Avro XIX G-AWRS, Valetta C.2 VX577 and many more. The small band have over the years developed NEAM into a regional collection to be proud of, with a careful restoration policy and an ever-expanding hangar/display hall building project. Their regard for XL319 is very apparent as the systems are all kept 'live', with the auxiliary power unit run-up on appropriate occasions

Above Two interesting 'zaps' on the nosewheel door of NEAM's XL319. The playful Goose Bay, Labrador, sticker is much more easily explained than is the Confederate Air Force stencilling! The Canadian base at Goose Bay was used by Vulcans as a detachment facility with a permanent RAF presence, and utilized by aircraft attending for low-level training in the area, or transitting to the USAF base at Offutt, Nebraska, for *Western Ranger* exercises. Now based at Midland, Texas, the Confederate Air Force were to be found further south in the 'Lone Star' state at Harlingen when XL319 was operational. It is possible they had their eyes on a Vulcan to join their then large static displays, and perhaps this is as close as they got to achieving such a goal!

Right Interesting angle on XL319's rear. The extreme end of the tail cone carries the radome of the Red Steer tail warning and ranging radar, and behind that to almost the rudder's trailing edge came a suite of powerful electronic countermeasures gear which was cooled from the intake duct shown to starboard. Above all of this was the braking parachute, which emerged from an upward-hinging door just behind the rudder's trailing edge

XL360 – Coventry

There have been few Vulcans documented carrying names operationally, No IX Sqn's *Mayflower III* being perhaps the only example (although there are many instances of 'nose-art' adorning the crew access door), but today the Midland Air Museum's (MAM) XL360 carries on the tradition of naming bombers after towns that have 'sponsored' them. During World War 2 the City of Coventry provided four aircraft for the RAF, and all carried the name of the city on their flanks. A ceremony at the MAM facility, Coventry Airport, Warwickshire, in August 1984 saw XL360 officially named *City of Coventry*, the occasion being overseen by the city's mayor, Councillor Walter Brandish, and overflown by Vulcan Display Team (VDT) B.2 XL426. Acquired through similar means as those utilized to buy a wartime bomber, MAM achieved their Vulcan by public subscription. XL360 last served with No 44 Sqn, and made its delivery flight from Waddington to Coventry Airport on 4 February 1983. Without a doubt, XL360 contributed much to the expansion of MAM at Coventry Airport, not just in size of exhibit, but more importantly in the pulling power that is evidently part and parcel of the Vulcan's charisma, be it operational, or statically displayed. MAM attribute the increase in visitors during the mid-1980s very much to the Vulcan, and it has helped in no small way in allowing the museum to grow into a major regional collection, boasting a fine aircraft display hall and many exhibits both large and small. XL360 was delivered out of Woodford on 1 March 1962, and served with No 617 Sqn and the Scampton Wing before joining No 230 OCU. The latter unit was the first taste that Vulcan aircrew got of the mighty delta, and here they worked up, ready to join an operational squadron. The OCU was formed at Waddington in late 1955 and took its first B.1s on in July of the following year. The unit moved to Waddington in July 1960, where it begun to receive its first B.2s. No 230 OCU moved to Finningley in June 1961, the unit staying in Yorkshire until December 1969, when it moved to Scampton, where it disbanded on 1 September 1981. After the OCU, XL360 served respectively with the Waddington Wing, No 230 OCU and Nos 617, 35 and 101 Sqns

Above Partial view of the rearward facing console for, left to right, navigator, radar plotter and air electronics officer. A seat for a sixth person (on the *Black Buck* missions this was an air refuelling specialist) is carried behind this bench and behind the pilots over the crew access door. Seats for the 'backroom boys' are termed as 'assisted exit seats', allowing for rapid exit downwards through the access door. With three (perhaps four) fully kitted flight crew in this area, co-ordination of movement was vital

Left The helm. Just a couple of sensitive deletions are to be found in the cockpit of XL360 at Coventry. All the 1982 and 1983 deliveries were left in remarkably good internal condition by the RAF. While this view clearly shows the instruments and controls, it does not really convey the cramped conditions when pilot and co-pilot are in place and in their full flying gear. Only the pilots had ejection seats

XL391 – Blackpool

The Manchester Vulcan Bomber Society's B.2 XL391 in reflective mood at the entrance to Blackpool Airport, Lancashire. XL391 was one of the 'chosen few' that deployed to Wideawake airfield on Ascension Island in May 1982 to take part in the amazing *Black Buck* strikes on the Falklands. The main story of the raids is best told by XM597, XM598 and XM607. As XL391 was a bridesmaid and not a bride for the operation, here is an appropriate place to set the scene for *Black Buck*. When *Operation Corporate* got under way, it was clear that the forces lacked long range, and heavy clout. It fell to No 44 Sqn at Waddington to supply this for the South Atlantic Force, and the base became a haven of industry and invention as the Vulcan was honed for a task it had never undertaken in anger, and for which current crews were not trained. Ten airframes were to be fitted up to standard, and in-flight refuelling (IFR) probes were scrounged from most of the already preserved Vulcans, including those at Goose Bay and Castle Air Force Base. Once fitted, training needed to get under way immediately - crews had not 'tanked' for a decade or more. The bomb-bays needed modifying, as for the anti-airfield role they would pack 'dumb' (or 'iron') bombs for a raid profile that would look much more like that of the Vulcan's illustrious forebear, the Lancaster. A Carousel inertial navigation system (INS), courtesy of British Airways, would also need to be fitted. On pylons fabricated at Waddington, an AN/ALQ-101D electronic countermeasures (ECM) pod would be carried to starboard, with the gear lashed up on the Air Electronic Officer's bench, next to the INS. A pylon on the port wing would take an AS.37 Martel anti-radar missile for self-protection, but in the end the US-made AGM-45A Shrike anti-radiation missile would be used, mounted on twin launchers fitted in the field at Wideawake. All this effectively started rolling on 8 April 1982, the first Vulcans touching down at Ascension 20 days later! The 'chosen few' turned out to be XL391, XM597, XM598, XM607, XM612 and XM654, these being deemed as the best in the operational fleet, having been taken from Nos 44 and 50 Sqns and the residue of the wound-down Nos IX and 101 Sqns. XM654 was soon eliminated from the fleet as it did not have the hard point attachments on the wings that were to carry the missiles and ECM gear. These originated in the days when the Vulcan B.2 was to carry the GAM-87A Skybolt long range stand-off weapon in 1961 following the demise of the Blue Streak inter-continental ballistic missile. Skybolt was cancelled by the USA and Britain opted for Polaris as the new deterrent. XL391 started life with the Ministry of Aviation trials fleet before moving on to the Bomber Command Development Unit (BCDU) at Finningley. BCDU undertook a wide range of developmental tasks, principally on bombing and navigation equipment, evaluating their use and tactics in a near 'operational' manner. From BCDU, XL391 moved on to serve within the Nos IX/35 Sqn pool, and with Nos 44, 101 and finally 44 Sqns. After *Corporate*, XL391 returned to Waddington and No 44 Sqn until the unit's disbandment in December 1982. The Manchester Vulcan Bomber Society secured the bomber by tender, and Blackpool Airport was chosen as its base, initially with optimistic ideas that they could operate the delta under a civilian aegis. XL391 flew into Blackpool Airport on 16 February 1983 and has been on public view ever since

Right Nose of XL391 showing the patterns that even Lancashire rain can create! The extreme nose 'thimble' houses the Ferranti terrain following radar, and above this can be seen the blanked off orifice that would have housed the in-flight refuelling probe. XL391 had one refitted for *Corporate*, but lost it again soon afterwards as the probe could also be fitted to the Nimrod and VC10

XL426 – Southend

Above Following retirement from the VDT, XL426 was offered for tender during the summer of 1986 and was sold to Vulcan zealot Roy Jacobsen. Roy had already purchased B.2 XM655 and this had been delivered to the airfield at Wellesbourne Mountford, Warwickshire, during February 1984. Roy was determined to operate a Vulcan under civilian auspices either alongside the VDT, or beyond the RAF's ultimate retirement of the type, and had decided that XL426 represented a much better chance of achieving this ambitious goal from both an age and engineering point of view. Roy formed the Vulcan Memorial Flight (VMF) for this purpose and soon a flourishing VMF Supporters' Club was established,

fundraising and generally making people aware of the limited service life left on the VDT Vulcan. XL426 was ferried from Waddington to Southend Airport, Essex, on 11 December 1986. Southend was a good choice of base as there were a number of major engineering companies on site who were capable of looking after an aircraft such as the Vulcan. On 7 July 1987 the aircraft was placed on the British civil register as G-VJET, in Roy's name, trading as the VMF. Registering an aircraft on the civil register is a comparatively simple task (a manhole cover was granted a civil registration once, just to prove how easy it was!), but the job of negotiating for something as complex and large as a Vulcan on a Permit to Fly or similar flying authorisation has yet to be achieved. At Southend, XL426

has been inspected and looked after by VMF Supporters' Club volunteers with an eye on its health and potential to fly. In recent times the VMF has been a major part of the astounding petitioning and campaigning centred around the decision to withdraw XH558 from the show circuit during 1992. Continuing its support and monitoring role into 1993, the VMF Supporters' Club will be watching the paths XH558 may take with great interest

Above Original badge of the Vulcan display flight, as carried on the crew access/escape door of B.2 XL426 at Southend

XM569 – Cardiff

Above With the removal from RAF St Athan of B.2 XM602 in mid-1992 (it had been earmarked for use by a property developer and may yet 'resurface' in one architectural form or another), XM569 at the Wales Aircraft Museum (WAM) at Cardiff-Wales Airport (or Rhoose) now alone holds the torch for the type in the Principality. WAM also have the nose section of B.1 XA903, best known for its time as the RB.199 test-bed, but also used for cannon and Blue Steel trials. Initially delivered to No 27 Sqn at Scampton on 31 January 1963, XM569 moved the following year to Cottesmore, Rutland, to join Nos IX and 35 Sqns in the base wing, where it lost unit markings as part of the centralised maintenance programme. No 35

Sqn had previously flown the Canberra B.2, taking on their first Vulcan B.2s at Coningsby in January 1963. The unit flew the Vulcan B.2 up to February 1982 when it disbanded. During that time No 35 Sqn lived a somewhat migratory life, moving to Cottesmore in November 1964, Akrotiri in February 1969 and to Waddington in January 1975. Beyond the Cottesmore Wing, XM569 joined the Waddington Wing and ended up with No 44 Sqn, also at Waddington, until disbandment in December 1982. Offered for tender, XM569 was snapped up by WAM and it was ferried to Cardiff-Wales Airport on 2 February 1983, joining WAM's extensive collection of aircraft which includes T-33A 29963, Buccaneer S.1 XN928 and Viscount 802 G-AOJC

Above Rear aspect of XM569 at the WAM facility, showing the exhausts of the Olympus engines with the cowlings temporarily removed. The City of Lincoln shield has faded somewhat, but the No 44 Sqn badge is well evident. The unit's official badge is an elephant, but with No 27 Sqn monopolising that motif, the unit opted instead for a double-four logo, probably wisely!

XM594 – Newark

Above Dominating the Newark Air Museum (NAM) at the Show Ground, Winthorpe, to the east of Newark, Nottinghamshire, is Vulcan B.2 XM594. The Vulcan touched down on the former bomber airfield, by then in use for gliding only, in a snow flurry on 7 February 1983. As with each of the airborne 'deliveries' in the first months of 1983, the ferry flight crew had carefully evaluated the runway long before and waited until conditions were as good as they could be. XM594 was acquired for NAM by benefactor Stuart Stephenson, who also bought several other museum 'heavyweights'. With nearly 50 aircraft on site and a huge aircraft display hall,

Newark has become a major place of pilgrimage. Restoration of the airframes is undertaken by a combination of work by full-time curator Mike Smith and members volunteering their time. Taking on the awesome prospect of an external refurbishment of XM594 during 1991 and into 1992 was NAM's Membership Secretary, Terry Musson. Terry segmented the airframe into 'manageable parts, otherwise I'd find the task too daunting' and set to, making sure that all of the underside was slotted for the winter of 1991/1992, giving him a large (triangular!) covered area to work under! XM594 was delivered to No 27 Sqn at Scampton from Avro's at Woodford on 9 July 1963, the bomber then joining No 617

Sqn also at Scampton, and later the centralised base wing. Final service came with No 44 Sqn at Waddington, XM594 staying at home while the five *Black Buck* examples deployed to Ascension Island. The veteran bomber was offered for tender during the summer of 1982

Above As the design of the Type 698 crystalised, it became clear that the Bristol Olympus engines would have to be buried deep within the wing and be supplied with copious amounts of air from large bifurcated ducts located in the leading edge close to the pressure bulkhead where the crew compartment lay. This necessitated intakes that swept in the same degree as the wing itself. The intake size was such that inspections of the 'tunnel' could be made by a nimble member of the groundcrew, equipped with a torch

XM597 – East Fortune

Left Vulcans have paid many overseas visits on 'flag waving' sorties, or long-ranging exercises, but the visit of XM597 to Galeas Air Base, Rio de Janeiro, Brazil, on 2 June 1982 was by far the most momentous, hitting the headlines the world over. This was the third of XM597's *Black Buck* missions. With limited manpower, aircraft parking facilities and above all limited tanking resources for such ambitious bombing missions, the *Black Buck* missions flown from Wideawake were to be 'solo' operations. A 'Primary' and 'Reserve' aircraft and crew were to be mustered for each sortie, but only one would go on to the target once it was proved which aircraft was truly operational. The number of Victor K.2 tankers that would be needed, in waves, to fuel the Vulcan outbound to the Falklands and then inbound to Wideawake was stretching the RAF's Victor force to the limit, with at times tankers topping tankers so that they themselves could reach the far-flung Vulcan. First mission for XM597 was *Black Buck 4*, with the aircraft slotted as the 'Primary' on 28/29 May. Argentinian radar sites around Port Stanley were the target, with both pylons toting 'twin-packs' of AGM-54A Shrike anti-radiation missiles. Crew was captain Sqn Ldr Neil McDougall; co-pilot F/O Chris Lackham; radar nav plotter Flt Lt Dave Castle; nav plotter Flt Lt Barry Smith; air electronics officer (AEO) Flt Lt Rod Trevaskus and air-to-air refuelling instructor (AARI) Flt Lt Brian Gardner. The AARI was from the Victor tanker force and swapped with the co-pilot when a top-up was due, advising and guiding the pilot – Vulcan crews had long since stopped training on in-flight refuelling. *Black Buck 4* aborted after a Victor went unserviceable when the entire 'circus' was not overly far from the tiny South Atlantic target. The whole raid (same crews, same aircraft) was rescheduled as *Black Buck 5* for the night of 30/31 May. The Vulcan was to time its arrival to co-incide with a Sea Harrier strike so that the Argentinians would be forced to use their radar, allowing *Black Buck 5*'s AEO to get a 'fix' that would permit the Shrikes to do their work. Three AGM-54As were launched but damage assessment could not be undertaken. The same combination of crews and aircraft was put together for the night of 2/3 June as *Black Buck 6*. This was another four-up Shrike mission, but this time with a low level profile followed by a sharp pull up in the hope of tempting the radar stations to 'illuminate' the Vulcan; throughout the sortie no air cover would be available. Two Shrikes were fired and it is thought one did indeed damage the principal radar site. The hook-up with the Victor after the raid ended in disaster with the in-flight refuelling probe fractured. Without a hope of continuing to the next tanker, XM597 set course for Rio, the only possible diversion airfield. Naturally, it would have been of great help to the Brazilians if the aircraft was not armed, so the Shrikes were jettisoned. One of the missiles refused to go and was to cause many diplomatic red faces when XM597 landed at Galeas with virtually dry tanks. The crew and aircraft were 'held' for a week,

then released back to Ascension. For XM597 the war was over! When the bomber undertook its *Black Buck* raids it had been in service with the RAF for 18 years and 10 months, having been initially delivered from Woodford to No 12 Sqn at Coningsby on 27 August 1963. No 12 Sqn started Vulcan operations with B.2s in July 1962, having last operated the Canberra B.6. The unit moved to Cottesmore in November 1964, and stayed there until disbanding in December 1967. In October 1969 the unit reformed with another legendary bomb mover, the Buccaneer S.2. From No 12 Sqn, XM597 was to serve respectively with the Waddington Wing, Nos 35, 50, IX, 101, 35 and 50 Sqns, ending its days with the Waddington Wing. With its history, the bomber was one of the first Vulcans earmarked for preservation, and it flew to East Fortune airfield, Lothian, Scotland, on 12 April 1984 to join the impressive Museum of Flight, part of the National Museums of Scotland

Left The markings on the nose of XM597 at East Fortune depict the bomber's two AGM-54A Shrike anti-radiation missile launches and its famous diversion to Rio de Janeiro at the end of *Black Buck 6*

XM598 – Cosford

Left When XM598 landed on the small runway at Cosford on 20 January 1983 following a brief delivery flight from Waddington to the Aerospace Museum at the RAF Station, it was a frustrated warhorse. Part of the 'chosen few' for the *Black Buck* missions from Ascension Island, it was mostly the stand-in. The bomber's one bid for fame – the very first mission – had XM598 filling the 'Primary' slot, but it went unserviceable and had to abort. *Black Buck 1*, on the night of 30 April/1 May 1982 had the runway at Port Stanley airfield in its sights. Shortly after take-off, XM598 went 'tech' and the 'Reserve' took its place. For *Black Buck 2* (3/4 May) XM598 was reserve to XM607 and from then it was understudy to XM597 for the aborted *Black Buck 4* (28/29 May), *Black Buck 5* (30/31 May) and *Black Buck 6* (2/3 June). Delivered to No 12 Sqn at Coningsby on 3 September 1963, XM598 went on to serve with both the Cottesmore and Waddington Wings, before ending its career with No 44 Sqn, the *Black Buck* detachment, and then the disbanding of the unit in December 1982. Allocated to the huge Aerospace Museum at Cosford, XM598 was given the maintenance airframe number 8778M upon arrival. Cosford is home to many aircraft, including types such as the Belfast, which puts even the Vulcan in the shade!

Above Chinagraph writing on the port visor of XM598 warns of a possible return to service. Signed by the captain, Sqn Ldr John Reeve (*Black Buck 2*), it says 'Delivered to the Museum on the same day Argentina moved squadrons of Mirages south towards the Falklands'. When XM598 touched down at Cosford, things were far from settled in the South Atlantic, although the war had been won. The deployment south by the Argentine Air Force was a worrying move and prompted the following note left on the starboard visor 'Please treat it with care. We may need it again in the South Atlantic'. Crew names for the ferry from Waddington to Cosford are also recorded: Sqn Ldr Reeve, Sqn Ldr Neil McDougall (*Black Bucks 4, 5* and *6*), Flt Lt Davies and Flt Lt Fletton

Right XM598's bomb-bay, showing an auxiliary fuel tank, which could carry 8000 lbs (3600 kg) of additional fuel. During the *Black Buck* missions the bay accommodated AGM-54A Shrike missiles and not a belly full of 'iron' bombs, two of these overload tanks could be carried, cutting down the number of air-to-air refuelling top-ups needed

XM603 – Woodford

Above XM603 is readily recognisable from all other Vulcans, the team at Woodford having repainted it in anti-flash white colours (using gloss to help in long term preservation and opting for full-shade red and blue on the roundels, not the more accurate pale shades). To add to the 'period' look, gone are the in-flight refuelling probe, nose-mounted terrain following radar 'thimble' and the fin tip-mounted passive electronic countermeasures package. Flown 'home' on 12 March 1982 from Waddington, XM603 had amassed some 5733 flying hours by the final touchdown. It was quickly to play a vital, but unsung, role in the looming Falklands

conflict. From 30 April, XM603 was used to try out the installation and 'plumbing' that was to lead to the K.2 tanker version, and later to try out other 'fixes' for the *Black Buck* aircraft. On 3 December 1963, XM603 started a journey away from Woodford that was to ultimately bring it back 20 years later, when the bomber was delivered off test to No IX Sqn at Coningsby. No IX operated Canberra B.6s before taking on Vulcan B.2s in April 1962. The unit flew Vulcans until disbanding in April 1982, operating from Cottesmore from November 1964, Akrotiri from February 1969 and Waddington from January 1975. With the bat symbol proudly displayed, No IX Sqn was back in June 1982, this time flying the

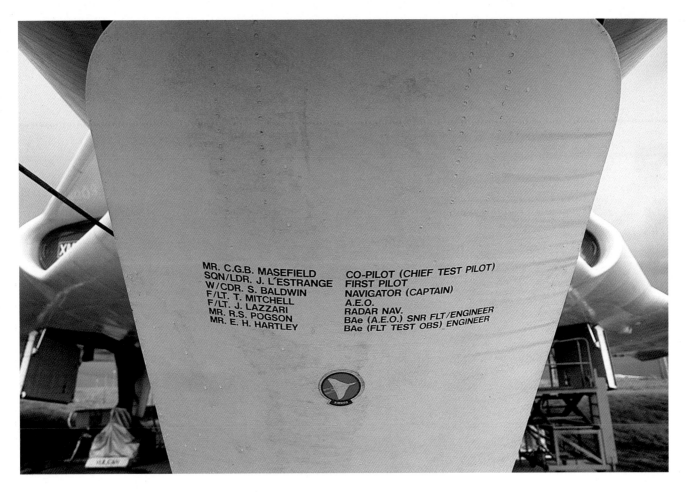

MR. C.G.B. MASEFIELD   CO-PILOT (CHIEF TEST PILOT)
SQN/LDR. J. L'ESTRANGE   FIRST PILOT
W/CDR. S. BALDWIN   NAVIGATOR (CAPTAIN)
F/LT. T. MITCHELL   A.E.O.
F/LT. J. LAZZARI   RADAR NAV.
MR. R.S. POGSON   BAe (A.E.O.) SNR FLT/ENGINEER
MR. E. H. HARTLEY   BAe (FLT TEST OBS) ENGINEER

Panavia Tornado GR.1. The aircraft also served with the Scampton and Waddington Wings, No 101 Sqn and finally No 44 Sqn. British Aerospace had long expressed the wish to have a Vulcan back at Woodford, and XM603 was the airframe chosen as a reminder of Avro's bomber prowess

Above As annotated on XM603's crew access door, the ferry flight from Waddington to Woodford on 12 March 1982 was a combined RAF and BAe affair. First pilot was Sqn Ldr Joe L'Estrange; co-pilot was Charles Masefield, then chief test pilot for BAe Woodford and now in charge of the Commercial Aircraft Division; navigator and captain for the flight was Wg Cdr S Baldwin; AEO Flt Lt Mitchell; radar nav plotter Flt Lt J Lazarri, the second AEO was R S Pogson, BAe's senior flight test engineer; and E H Hartley, BAe flight test observer, acted as engineer in what must have been a crowded cockpit!

XM607 Waddington

Left Final home to operational Vulcans, and to XH558, it is fitting that Waddington should have a Vulcan as 'gate' guardian and that it be an illustrious example. XM607 was delivered to the RAF on the last day of 1963, joining No 35 Sqn at Coningsby, then No 101 Sqn at Waddington, before settling down with No 44 Sqn, also at the latter base. After the Falklands conflict, XM607 stayed on charge with No 44 Sqn to its disbandment in December 1982, and during 1983 was placed on display within the camp, being allocated the maintenance serial number 8779M. One of the five airframes allocated for the *Black Buck* operations, it was modified and ferried to Wideawake airfield. *Black Buck 1* was to be the first raid on the runway at Port Stanley Airfield and was conducted on the night of 30 April/1 May 1982. XM598 was the 'Primary' and XM607 was 'Reserve'. Both were loaded up with 21 1000-lb (454 kg) high explosive bombs, some fitted with a variety of delay fuzes. The target was not an easy one, but if all went well the airfield would still be suffering cataclysmic explosions up to one hour after the raid. The Argentine forces would also realise that the long arm of the UK was reaching out to them. Both Vulcans took off, but XM598 suffered a malfunction and it fell to Flt Lt Martin Withers as captain; F/O Peter Taylor as co-pilot; Flt Lt Bob Wright as nav radar plotter; Flt Lt Gordon Graham as navigator; Flt Lt Hugh Prior as AEO and Flt Lt Richard Russell as AARI to undertake the first in the sequence of the longest ever bombing raids in the history of aerial warfare – 15 hours 45 minutes flight time. No less than 11 Handley Page Victor K.2 tankers were needed for the operation, and on the leg to Stanley one of the final two Victors suffered a fractured probe, requiring the aircraft to swap over roles of 'mother' and 'receiver'. Victor K.2 XL189, which undertook the final run in with XM607, was preserved alongside XM607 on the gate at Waddington, providing a fitting memorial to the *Black Buck* raids. Sadly it had to go as part of the MoD's one-gate, one guardian policy, and it was scrapped in September 1989. On the run into Stanley, *Black Buck 1*, came down to 300 ft (90 m) to avoid Argentine radar, before 'popping up' to 10,000ft (3050m) for the bomb run. For *Black Buck 2* on 3/4 May XM607 was 'Primary' with XM598 as 'Reserve'. The bomb-bay again carried 21 1000-pounders, with the airfield installations at Stanley as the target. Crew for this mission was Sqn Ldr R J Reeve (captain), Flt Lt D T Dibbins (co-pilot); Flt Lt M A Cooper (nav radar); Flt Lt J Vinales (nav); Flt Lt Barry Masefield (AEO - Barry went on to be AEO with the VDT in the final days of XH558) and Flt Lt P Standing (AARI). XM607 was 'Primary' again for *Black Buck 3*, set for 12/13 May. XM612 was 'Reserve', but in the end the mission was scrubbed due to weather. With its bomb-bay set up for 'iron' bombs in profusion, XM607 was not used on *Black Bucks 4, 5* and *6*, being held back for the final raid, which again needed conventional bombs. Staged during the night of 11/12 June, *Black Buck 7* had XM607 (with the same crew

as *Black Buck 1*) as 'Primary' with XM612 again as
'Reserve'. In the bomb-bay were 1000-pounders and air
burst fuzed anti-personnel weapons; XM607 was to attack
troop concentrations around Port Stanley as British troops
yomped across the island for the final showdown. It was
difficult to assess the damage inflicted by the raid, but the
psychological effect must have been enormous on an
already demoralised, and largely conscript, ground force.
During the Gulf War, USAF B-52 Stratofortresses were
used in similar long-ranging missions with air burst
weaponry against Iraqi troop concentrations, doubtless
taking a leaf out of *Black Buck 7*'s book

Above Nose of XM607 showing the very modest mission
tallies for the three *Black Buck* missions the aircraft
undertook (Raids *1, 2* and *7*).

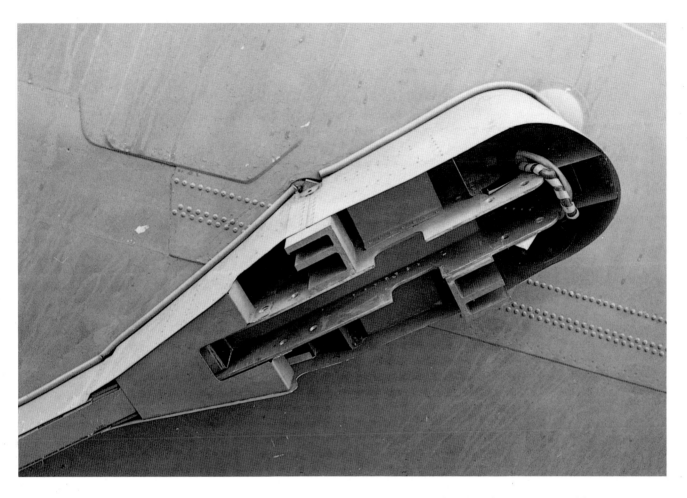

Above Displayed within the camp at Waddington, XM607 carries examples of the somewhat 'agricultural' pylons built at the base in April 1982 for the *Black Buck* Vulcans. In conventional bombing operations (as undertaken by XM607 on *Black Bucks 1, 2* and *7*), weapon load on the pylons was an AN/ALQ-101D electronic countermeasures pod to starboard and a 'twin-pack' of AGM-54A Shrike anti-radiation missiles on the port. For the dedicated anti-radar missions (*Black Bucks 4, 5* and *6*) two Shrikes were carried on each pylon (*Alan Curry*)

XM612 – Norwich

Above Travellers flying Air UK out of Norwich Airport, Norfolk (one time Horsham St Faith airfield), must frequently wonder what the small collection of aircraft huddled on the north side are, particularly as one of them looks like a Vulcan. It is a Vulcan, and it is the flagship of the City of Norwich Aviation Museum. The collection includes Herald 211 G-ASKK, as once operated by Air UK from the airport, and Javelin FAW.9 XH767 as flown from the airfield in the late 1950s. While Vulcans were not known as East Anglian animals, it gets by far the most attention when the museum is opened to the public of a weekend. XM612 was delivered to Coningsby on 2 March

1964, joining the resident No IX Sqn. From there it went on to serve with both the Scampton and the Waddington Wings, before joining the decentralised No 44 Sqn at the latter base. XM612 was selected to be a *Black Buck* aircraft in April 1982, and deployed to Ascension Island. The bomber was destined never to embark upon an offensive mission but was slated twice as 'Reserve', although launched only once in this back-up role. For *Black Buck 3*, XM612 was 'Reserve' to 'Primary' XM607, but the mission was scrubbed. For the final raid, *Black Buck 7*, XM612 was again 'Reserve' to XM607's 'Primary' - both took off loaded with conventional 1000-pounders and air burst weapons, but it was XM607 that flew on and XM612 that

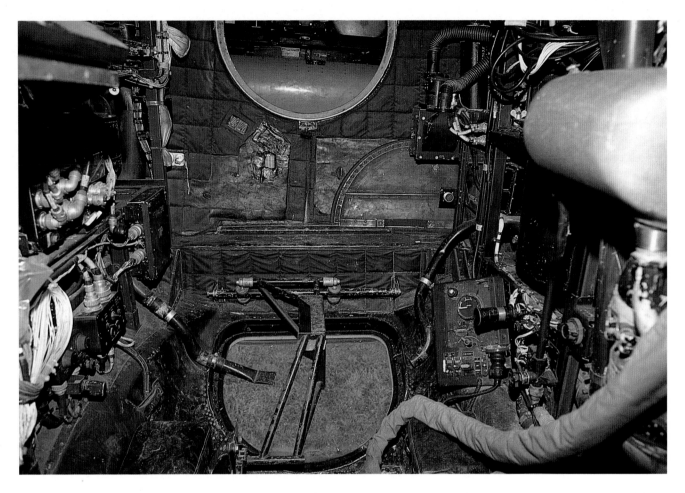

turned back to Wideawake. Put up for tender during the summer of 1982, XM612 was secured by the City of Norwich Aviation Museum through the generosity of John Hale, who acquired the Vulcan on their behalf. It flew from Waddington to Norwich Airport on 30 January 1983

Above When the Vulcan B.1 was instigated, the need for bomb aiming via the then traditional viewpoint of a prone bomb aimer was still required. Hence the aircraft was built with a bomb aimer's position underneath the crew area. On the B.2 this position was never kitted out and was a reminder of days gone by

XM655 – Wellesbourne Mountford

Above Adding scale to the Cessna 152s and other light aircraft that fly from the former Wellington bomber training base at Wellesbourne Mountford, Warwickshire, is Vulcan XM655, the youngest survivor. Third to last off the Woodford production line, it was delivered to the RAF on 20 November 1964, joining No IX Sqn at Cottesmore. No IX had only moved in from Coningsby ten days before. Beyond service with this unit came a first stint with No 44 Sqn, then Nos 50 and 101 Sqns, before returning to No 44 again at Waddington. When the squadron disbanded in December 1982, XM655 was kept current at Waddington and released for sale by tender the following year. It was XM655 that first attracted the eye of

Vulcan advocate Roy Jacobsen, and, having acquired it from the MoD, he arranged to have the aircraft ferried to Wellesbourne Mountford on 11 February 1984. Sixteen days later Roy placed the bomber on the British civil register as G-VULC, his dream being to operate a Vulcan under civil auspices via the Vulcan Memorial Flight, an organisation he founded at about the same time. In September 1985 Roy transferred the Vulcan to the US civil register as N655AV (*November-six-five-fiver-AVro*) in the hope that US documentation would enable the Vulcan to fly with greater ease than it seemed possible under UK Civil Aviation Authority rulings. During 1986 the founder VDT aircraft, XL426 came up for disposal and Roy was successful in acquiring that as well. It was flown into

Southend Airport on 11 December 1986. From then on it was XL426 that was to receive the attention and XM655 continued to stand at Wellesbourne, gathering a hefty amount in parking fees. During 1992 the owners of the airfield, Radar Moor Ltd, were forced to take up a County Court action for the outstanding fees on XM655. Less than an hour before the case was due to be heard, an out of court settlement found Radar Moor as owners of XM655 for the princely sum of £1! Newly-formed is the Delta Engineering Association, a group of specialists who aim to restore the aircraft to full ground running capability

Above Just discernible on the fin of XM655 at Wellesbourne Mountford are the twin greyhounds used as an unofficial badge by No 50 Sqn. XM655 served with No 50 two units back, having spent time with Nos 101 and 44 Sqns since then. Despite this, when delivered to Wellesbourne in February 1984 it was No 50's badge that adorned the fin. Above it can be discerned the shield of the City of Lincoln

Below Barksdale Air Force Base, Bossier City, Louisiana, is home to the Eighth Air Force Museum and was to host a whole series of bombing competitions held between the USAF's Strategic Air Command and the RAF's Bomber (later Strike) Command. It is thus a very fitting place for a Vulcan, and XM606 was delivered there on 9 June 1982. This aircraft entered RAF service on 20 December 1963, and flew with No 12 Sqn, the Cottesmore Wing, Ministry of Aviation trials fleet and the Akrotiri and Waddington Wings respectively. Proudly 'flying' the Union Flag on the fin – the garb worn by all Vulcans taking part in the *Giant Voice* competitions – XM606 is appropriately illustrated at Barksdale in November 1974 *(L B Sides via David F Brown)*

Right Final Vulcan delivery to the USA came just seven days after XM606 touched down in Louisiana, with the delivery of XM573 to Offutt Air Force Base, the home of SAC, near Omaha, Nebraska. Delivered to the RAF on 27 March 1963, XM573 served with No 83 Sqn, the Waddington Wing, No 230 OCU, the Akrotiri and Waddington Wings, No 230 OCU and finally No 44 Sqn. Offutt was a frequent deployment for Vulcans on *Western Ranger* navigation and low flying deployments, and is also home to a large museum dedicated to the history of SAC. Illustrated during July 1989, XM573 was then undergoing a programme of refurbishment by British ex-pat volunteers

First and last – XH588

Right Founder-member of the VDT at Waddington was XL426. For the 1984 and 1985 seasons this Vulcan performed at a select number of airshows and was operated in an entirely volunteer manner. In 1986 XH558, the first Vulcan B.2 to be delivered to the RAF and the last on operational charge, took over. After a successful season, it was obvious while the mighty Vulcan was undergoing maintenance in 'its' hangar at Waddington that the VDT needed a more formalised arrangement with its groundcrew - a full-time team was needed. A request was made for seven groundcrew from all of the trades needed to operate a Vulcan, and look after it so that engineering skills and experience acquired could be capitalised on. The 1987 summer season was undertaken on the totally volunteer basis of previous years while the results of the request were awaited

Above right At the beginning of the 1988 airshow season the request for full-time maintenance personnel was granted and the continued operation of XH558 was assured, at least from an engineering point of view. The engineering officer, Officer Commanding Engineering and Supply Wing at Waddington and occasional specialist engineers remained volunteers, seeing to the needs of XH558 when their other duties allowed and in their spare time. Engineering responsibility for the Vulcan came directly from No 11 Group Headquarters, Stanmore, Greater London. VDT groundcrew team for the 1992 season were Flt Lt Pat McGeough (Engineering Officer); Chief Tech Ben Davis (Groundcrew Team Leader); Chief Tech Dave Thorpe (Crew Chief); Sgt Barry Todd (Electrician); Cpl Charlie Gray (Airframes); Cpl Taff Stone (Electrician); Cpl John Lambert (Propulsion); Cpl Jim Clancy (Avionics); Sgt Terry Kilby (Avionics); and Sgt Tom Selby (Airframes). With XH558 as the sole remaining operational aircraft, consumable spares were sought out from all over the RAF and brought to a central store at Waddington. Replacements for many items in the Vulcan's inventory would simply not be possible once stocks were consumed – it would be out of the question to commission further, necessarily small, batches. The future of XH558 depended not just on care and attention to all maintenance schedules, but to precise calculations of consumption of major items, sparing use of flying hours and a constant search for hitherto 'lost' spares caches. It was quite conceivable that something as lowly as the tyre stocks could ground the 'mighty delta' forever

Right Inside the intake of XH558's port outer Olympus 301. Cpl Charlie Gray (Airframes) checks out the whole area for blemishes and damage. It is here and further back into the engines themselves that birdstrikes and foreign object damage (FOD) can wreak havoc. Thankfully, the Vulcan's long legs keep it well away from all but the most determined FOD, but not of course from members of the bird population! A damaged panel further down this intake duct took three days to repair, and involved changing an entire section of body work. Charlie first came to Waddington in July 1981 and worked in two sessions on the now abortive Nimrod AEW.3 programme, which had a Joint Trials Unit operating from the base. In his spare time he helped out with VDT, joining them officially in June 1987

Right In terms of the propulsion systems, the Vulcan was put together with an eye to a goodly degree of accessibility. With two plastic containers taking care of drainage, propulsion specialist Cpl John Lambert takes a look into the engine accessory bay. John first came to Waddington in 1981 to work with the base wing's Vulcans during their last months of operation. After a short spell at Honington, Suffolk, on Tornado GR.1s, John returned to Waddington to work with No 50 Sqn, now flying the Vulcan in the tanker role. A Spey Mk 250 turbofan propulsion course led to work with the Nimrod servicing section at the JTU, with John giving his time to XH558 to help with engine changes. John joined the VDT as a full-time member of the groundcrew in February 1989

Left XH558 operated out of the 1936/37-period hangars, which were borne in mind when the Specification that gave rise to the Vulcan was drawn up. The runway was lengthened to 9000 ft (2.8 km) during the reconstruction of the base to accept a Vulcan wing in the late 1950s, and the airfield itself is close on 1000 acres in area. Just to the south of Lincoln, Waddington has had a long and illustrious past. It was opened in 1916, eventually becoming No 48 Training Depot Station before closure in 1919. Aircraft to be seen around at this time included Avro 504s, de Havilland DH.4s and DH.9s and Royal Aircraft Factory RE.8s. The base re-opened in 1926 as the home of No 503 Sqn, a reserve unit. During the mid-1930s, the decision was taken to turn Waddington into a major bomber base, and the pattern was set to establish the base, and its size, much as it appears today. Among units reforming here in 1937 was No 50 Sqn, later to operate Vulcans from the base. Arriving in the same year was another unit to have great associations with the Vulcan, No 44 Sqn, this outfit becoming the first to take on Blenheim Is. With the start of World War 2 in September 1939, Nos 44 and 50 Sqns (both with Hampdens) went straight into action. In 1940/41 Nos 97 and 207 Sqns began to work up on the generally unsuccessful Manchester, but by December of that year it was the Lancaster that was to become the hallmark of the base for the remainder of the war, with No 44 Sqn accepting its first aircraft. No IX Sqn (another Vulcan user to be) moved in and converted to Lancasters also. In 1943 two Australian units arrived, Nos 463 and 467 Sqns. The latter unit flew the famous Lancaster *S-Sugar*/R5868 from the base and on to its record 100 sorties. This aircraft is preserved today at the RAF Museum, Hendon, in close proximity to Vulcan XL318. The RAAF squadrons were to remain as Waddington's principal units to the war's end. From 1946, the sound of Lancasters gave way to the sound of the Lincoln, operated by Nos 49, 57, 61 and 100 Sqns for varying times until the station was placed into Care and Maintenance in 1953. This was to prepare the base for its next task – home to V-bombers. For a brief while Nos 21 and 27 (another Vulcan unit in waiting) Sqns flew Canberra B.2s from Waddington. The first Vulcan B.1s arrived during 1956 for No 230 OCU, followed by No 83 Sqn – the RAF's first operational Vulcan unit – in May 1957. No 44 Sqn returned to Waddington in August 1960, with Vulcan-equipped Nos 101 and IX Sqns following soon after. With the phase-out of the Vulcan as a bomber completed by December 1982, and the disbanding of No 50 Sqn with its K.2 tankers in March 1984, the airfield settled down to await its new role as home for RAF's AEW force. The unit would be No 8 Sqn, then operating the venerable Shackleton AEW.2 from Lossiemouth in Scotland, and the new type was confidently expected to be the Nimrod AEW.3, with a JTU being established at the base to evaluate the new type. All of this resulted in massive delays when the RAF shifted its thoughts to the Sentry AEW.1, and No 8 Sqn finally took on the type operationally in July 1991, operating out of a huge new engineering hangar at the northern end of the airfield. The base is also very busy as the host of the British Aerospace-operated North Sea air combat manoeuvring range, with fighters from many European nations dropping in for training

Above From the hangar, XH558 is towed out to its dispersal alongside the control tower. Cpl John Lambert (left) and Sgt Barry Todd (right) assist Chief Tech Dave Thorpe, the VDT's Crew Chief, with the tow bar

Right 'Step inside'. The crew access door as seen from inside the cabin, looking aft to the nosewheels. In a bail-out the 'back seaters' would use this door as an emergency shoot to leave the aircraft

Above Out on the pastoral setting of the dispersal, ready for start up. The panther's head is the symbol of No 1 Group, RAF. The Group holds the responsibility for VDT flying operations, via the Officer Commanding the Victor K.2-equipped No 55 Sqn at Marham, Norfolk. The bulk of the flight crew have been drawn from this unit over the years

Right Lettering on the crew access door of XH558 during its final season, detailing the flightcrew and the groundcrew heads: Sqn Ldr Paul Millikin, captain; Sqn Ldr Dave Thomas, captain; Sqn Ldr Dave Moore, navigator; Sqn Ldr Ken Denman, air electronics officer (AEO); Sqn Ldr Barry Masefield, AEO; Flt Lt Al Slack, navigator; Flt Lt Dave Bradford, navigator; Flt Lt Stu Mitchell, co-pilot; Flt Lt Tim Walker, co-pilot; Flt Lt Graham O'Connor, navigator; Flt Lt Pat McGeough, engineering officer; Chief Tech Dave Thorpe, crew chief; Chief Tech Ben Davis, groundcrew leader

SQN LDR P MILLIKIN CAPT
SQN LDR D THOMAS CAPT
SQN LDR D MOORE NAV
SQN LDR K DENMAN AEO
SQN LDR B MASEFIELD AEO
FLT LT A SLACK NAV
FLT LT D BRADFORD NAV
FLT LT S MITCHELL PILOT
FLT LT T WALKER PILOT
FLT LT G O'CONNOR NAV
FLT LT P McGEOUGH ENG OFF
CHF TECH D THORPE ASC
CHF TECH B DAVIS I/C

DANGER
EJECTION
SEAT
DANGER DANGER

Above Port side of the navigation and air electronics bench – the domain of the 'back room boys' of the Vulcan. Facing aft, the specialist officers have two small portholes, port and starboard, to give them some form of reference point on the outside world. AEO Sqn Ldr Barry Masefield is sat at his 'office'. Barry joined the RAF in 1959 as a radar technician apprentice and he qualified as an AEO in 1963, going on to fly Shackletons in the maritime role from Ballykelly, Singapore and Honington, with detachments to Madagascar for the Beira patrol. In 1972 Barry converted to the Nimrod maritime patrol aircraft and flew with the Kinloss Wing in Scotland. In 1979 he was commissioned and joined the Vulcan force. Barry is no stranger to Waddington's gate guardian, Vulcan B.2 XM607; he was AEO on this aircraft for the *Black Buck 2* raid on Port Stanley airfield in May 1982. In 1983 Barry joined No 55 Sqn at Marham, flying the Victor K.2

Above right Start up at the Waddington dispersal. The heat shimmer behind the aircraft gives testament to the power of the four Bristol Olympus 301s, each of which delivers 20,000 lbs of static thrust. What the shot cannot convey is the awesome noise. Groundcrew members, well protected from the shattering din surrounding them, are still aware of the power of the aircraft. Despite the solid nature of the Lincolnshire Wolds and the good construction of Waddington's dispersals, it is possible to 'hear' the roar through the soles of the feet! Once the pre-flight checks are completed the Vulcan will taxy out to Waddington's only operational runway - the 'black top' is 9000 ft (2.8 km) long and aligned at right angles to the reshaped A15, which was moved to accommodate the runway extension needed when the base became a Vulcan lair

Right Chief Tech Ben Davis, Team Leader for the VDT's groundcrew, gives a presentation on the history of XH558 to visitors. Ben first met up with XH558 in 1980 when it was with No 27 Sqn; he moved to No 44 Sqn upon No 27's wind-down and so did XH558. Ben joined the VDT in 1991 and was often to be found chronicling the life and times of XH558 to the many visitors the VDT enjoyed

Above XH558 during its days with No 27 Sqn in the guise of a B.2(MRR), wearing high gloss camouflage when all the conventional Vulcan bomber fleet had opted for matt hues. Avro Type 698 Vulcan B.2 XH558 was ordered under MoD contract number 6/Acft/11301/Cb.6(a), placed on 30 September 1954, which called for 17 B.Mk 2 versions of the Avro Vulcan. XH558 was 'plumbed' for the abortive Douglas GAM-87A Skybolt long range nuclear stand-off weapon. Built at Avro's Woodford factory, near Stockport, XH558 was completed in 1960 and took to the air for the first time on 21 May. On 1 July 1960 it became the first Mk 2 to

enter RAF service when delivered to 'B' Flight of No 230 OCU at Waddington, where the bomber first trained No 83 Sqn crews, who subsequently went on to join their unit at Scampton. Transferred from Waddington to Finningley with the OCU on 16 June 1961, the Vulcan was to remain in Yorkshire for the next eight years until on 23 February 1968, when it returned to Waddington. Here, '558 became part of the Waddington Wing under the centralised servicing scheme until individual squadron allocations came into practice again and it joined No 101 Sqn on 31 October 1972, still at Waddington. The bomber was also flown by Nos 44 and

XH558 was one of three aircraft equipped to carry these pods, but not as a permanent fixture. On completion, it was delivered to No 27 Sqn at Scampton on 17 September 1974, and was used for maritime reconnaissance and air sampling, remaining current until 30 March 1982 when it returned to Waddington to join No 44 Sqn. With the beginning of the Falklands conflict (2 April to 14 June 1982), '558 was earmarked as one of six to be converted to the stop-gap tanker role and despatched to Woodford by July 1982 for conversion to K.2, which involved fitment of a hastily-installed hose drum unit mounted under the extreme rear fuselage. XH558 was the last of the six to be converted, and it was delivered back to Waddington on 12 October 1982, this time joining No 50 Sqn but moving on only two weeks later to the A&AEE at Boscombe Down on 25 October for tanking trials before heading back up north. During 1983, the refuelling gear from '558 was removed for use in the VC10 tanker conversion programme. On 17 September 1984, the aircraft was flown to Marham, pending disposal, but unlike the majority of the other Vulcans at this time which were scrapped, '558 was selected on 14 November 1984 for service with the VDT. Returned to Waddington, the bomber underwent a Service Embodied Modification (SEM) conversion by RAF engineers during the winter of 1984/85, flying once again in the spring in a configuration which mirrored its fitment during its operational V-Force days. Between September and November 1985, '558 was resprayed at RAF Kinloss in its current gloss camouflage, with the Lincoln coat of arms on the tail fin signifying freedom of the City of Lincoln, a Union Jack, and on either side of the fuselage forward of the intakes, the panther's head emblem of No 1 Group, Strike Command. These markings were chosen because they were carried by all Vulcans taking part in SAC's *Giant Voice* bombing and navigation competitions and are therefore representative of all Vulcan units during the 1970s. It returned to Waddington on completion of the respray on 30 November 1985, and the following May replaced previous VDT Vulcan XL386, making its airshow debut at the TVS event held at Bournemouth (*Military Aircraft Photographs*)

50 Sqns at Waddington, although no precise dates are recorded. XH558 left for Bitteswell, Leicestershire, on 17 August 1973, where Hawker Siddeley Aviation carried out conversion to B.2(MRR) maritime radar reconnaissance standard, including fitment of the forward and aft facing passive electronic countermeasures antennae atop the fin, removal of the terrain following radar 'thimble' installation of LORAN navigational equipment, and an array of electronic installations in the bomb-bay and elsewhere. Five B.2(MRR)s had fixed air sampling pods fitted to the long-redundant Skybolt hardpoints under the wing;

Above XH558 making a run into Marham. Operating the last flying examples of the shapely Victor, in the form of the K.2 tanker variant, No 55 Sqn is due to disband in October 1993 when the Victors will be sold off, with a few earmarked for museums. Marham is currently host to a Tornado GR.1 and GR.1A wing, comprising Nos II, 27 and 617 Sqns, the latter two having previously flown the Vulcan

Left On 7 September 1992, XH558 made a sortie on behalf of the media for a last-ever air-to-air session. Packed into a Lyneham tactical wing Hercules C.1, still and video cameras clicked away throughout the flight, which included a visit to Marham, XH558's 'operational' headquarters. There follows a portfolio of photographs taken on that sortie. Over home territory, XH558 flies over Waddington, with the huge Sentry AEW.1 maintenance hangar and three examples from the resident No 8 Sqn parked on the ramp. To the right, the A15 road snakes its way north to Lincoln. Behind XH558's fin and rudder are the Belfast truss hangars of the former Bracebridge Heath airfield. These hangars were used during World War 2 for the overhaul and repair of Lancasters, which were then trundled down the A15 to Waddington. Between 1951 and 1953 the Bracebridge Heath hangars were used to construct Avro 707s WZ736 and WZ744, both aircraft acting as scale aerodynamic test vehicles for the Vulcan programme, and both performing their first flights from Waddington

Above Adopted when the Vulcan moved to a low level attack profile in the mid- to late-1960s, at first with the modified Blue Steel stand-off weapon and then with conventional weaponry, the dark green and medium sea grey camouflage with light grey undersides can be seen to have a good effect even against the crop fields of Lincolnshire and East Anglia. The scheme worn by XH558 is somewhat of a 'timewarp', representing the Vulcans of the 1970s

Left A nose aspect of XH558 during the press sortie of 7 September 1992. The 'coke bottle', or area rule, method of streamlining is well evident, as is how little of the airframe is devoted to the crew

Above Wingspan of the Vulcan B.2 is 111 ft (33.8 m), with a length of 99 ft 11 in (30.5 m) and a massive wing area of 3965 ft^2 (368.3 m^2). Maximum speed at 40,000 ft (12,192 m) is 645 mph (1038 km/h), or a Mach number of 0.98

Right Now with the huge 'barn doors' deployed, two on each side of the top of the wing and one (just visible) under each side of the bottom. All carrying a 'no step' logo, the airbrakes run up and down on very industrial-looking stanchions and then fold flat to become part of the flying surface

Above On Wednesday 16 September 1992 Vulcan B.2 XH558 taxied out at Waddington for what might well have been officially the last time, as it was embarking on its last public appearances, with a flight down to the Channel Islands for Jersey and Guernsey's Battle of Britain celebrations, then a long positioning flight to Leuchars in readiness for their Battle of Britain 'At Home' show, then to Finningley for the second 'At Home' of the day, with an overnight before flying on to Cranfield, Beds, for the Dreamflight show – XH558's last ever public appearance. The Vulcan would make its return to home base on Monday 21 September. It was to be a hectic and emotional deployment. Duncan Cubitt took the following portfolio during XH558's visit to the Channel Islands. In the past the Vulcan had made the Islands' Battle of Britain days a 'flying visit' only, but this time, the Islanders were to be treated to the thrill of truly hosting the aircraft. On Wednesday 16 September the groundcrew got away in a No 6 Flying Training School (FTS) Jetstream T.1 at around 0900 hours, bound for Jersey Airport. The crew boarded XH558 at 1025 (it had been fuelled up the previous day)

and took off from Waddington, landing at Jersey, with braking 'chute streaming at about 1215. The following day, another groundcrew party set off on the trek to Leuchars, ready for the arrival of XH558 there

Above right The States Airport of Jersey was happy to lend a set of airliner steps to allow the braking parachute to be re-installed into its bay above what was the electronic countermeasures bay in the days when the aircraft was a bomber. Three 'chutes were carried, slung on a net system inside the bomb-bay, giving the deployment to the Channel Islands a great degree of self-sufficiency should a 'chute be damaged

Right XH558 shared the ramp at Jersey with the aircraft that was designed to succeed the Vulcan in the heavy strike role, the Tornado GR.1. These belong to No 27 Sqn, based at Marham, and a former user of the Vulcan

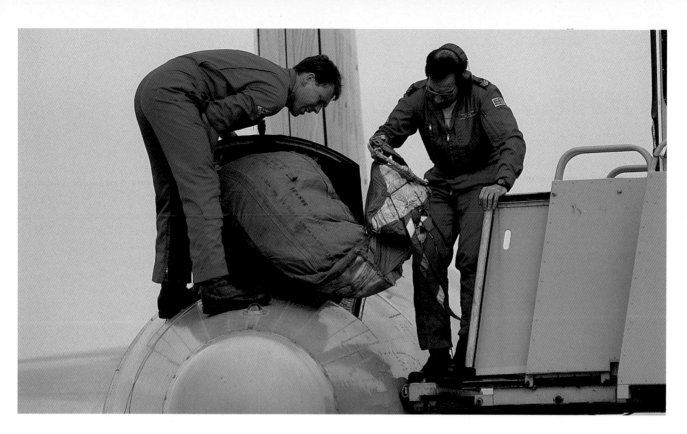

Above and left The 'Blues' and the 'Greens'. Vulcan crew had two uniforms, the classic RAF issue 'Greens', worn for most flights and training, and the 'Blues' for times when a more formal and 'showy' appearance was expected. Britain's military aviation magazine *Airforces Monthly* was proud to help the VDT groundcrew during the 1992 season with their 'Blues'. From left to right, the first crewman in the above photograph is Sqn Ldr Dave Thomas, a former Vulcan and display pilot for the type during its operational days. Dave joined the VDT in 1989 and was a display captain for the 1992 season. All aircrew on VDT are volunteers, Dave's day-to-day job being a flying instructor at the CFS at Scampton, flying the Tucano T.1. Next is Flt Lt Graham O'Connor, who volunteers his time as a navigator on XH558. He joined the RAF in 1985, going on to fly with No 55 Sqn at Marham on the Victor K.2. During 1992, Graham was serving as a navigator instructor with No 6 FTS at Finningley. Forever the diplomat, it is Graham's boast that his joining the VDT navigator team brought down their average age to a mere 63! Peering over his shoulder is fellow navigator Flt Lt Al Slack, who started his operational flying with the RAF on the Canberra TT.18 target tug with No 7 Sqn (whose unofficial motto was 'We aim to please, you aim too, please!') at St Mawgan, Cornwall. From there he gravitated to the PR.9 reconnaissance version of the Canberra before converting to the Vulcan, with No 101 Sqn at Waddington. Al then joined No 55 Sqn flying the Victor K.2, and that was still his posting during the 1992 season. Standing alongside him is Flt Lt Dave Bradford, who, having flown Valiants before joining the Vulcan force, spent time with the Nimrod AEW.3 JTU prior to converting onto the Victor K.2, a type he was still flying with No 55 Sqn during the 1992 season. Navigator Dave has therefore flown in all three of the V-bomber types. The fifth member of the team featured in this photograph is air electronics officer Sqn Ldr Barry Masefield. In 'Greens' left to right are Flt Lt Graham O'Connor, Flt Lt Al Slack, Sqn Ldr Paul Millikin (of which more anon!) and Sqn Ldr Barry Masefield

Above Even XH558's intake covers are an appreciable bit of kit! Braking parachute bag shown for size

Left VDT patch, including the panther's head of No 1 Group

Right It takes dedicated people to really love an aircraft. Crew Chief on XH558 is Chief Tech Dave Thorpe, seen here on the throat microphone 'umbilical' talking to the crew during some untypical Channel Island weather. Dave joined the RAF in 1962 at St Athan, Wales. After training he moved to Wyton, Huntingdonshire, on Victors and then on detachment to the Canadian base at Goose Bay, looking after transitting Victors and Vulcans. Next came time with Wessex and Whirlwind helicopters at Odiham, Hampshire, and then to Wittering, Cambs, on Whirlwinds, Hunters and the Harrier. Travels again took him to Singapore, back with the Wessex, then to Scampton and the resident Vulcan wing, before moving to piston power with the venerable Hastings T.5s of No 230 OCU from 1974 to 1979. In 1981 Dave became a Vulcan Crew Chief with No 50 Sqn at Waddington, staying with the tanker unit until it disbanded in March 1984, when he moved neatly across to become the VDT's hard working and dedicated Crew Chief

Above At around 1025 hours on Thursday 17 September, the crew got on board XH558, ready for a take-off from Jersey at 1125 for their display over Guernsey. Ground crew had started their work and checks on the aircraft from 0900

Right VDT's Engineering Officer shows a turn of heel at Jersey – and so he might as apart from the rain, Pat is a proficient cross-country runner. Flt Lt Pat McGeough was Officer Commanding Aircraft and Bays Maintenance Flight at Waddington during the 1992 season until a posting in December down to the Falklands. OC Aircraft and Bays Maintenance gave Pat a huge 'beat' to look after, including the Sentry AEW.1 force operated from Waddington by No 8 Sqn, sundry maintenance needs at the base, the visiting aircraft and engineering responsibility for XH558. Pat took to this work with a passion and greatly liked the other role that the post gave him; that of Flight Commander for the groundcrew. Pat joined the RAF in 1964, training as an engine mechanic. He served at Leconfield, Acklington, Cottesmore and Church Fenton in the UK, Khormaksar in Aden, Kai Tak in Hong Kong and Wildenrath in the former West Germany. This gave him experience of many types, including Dakota, Canberra, Andover, Pembroke, Twin Pioneer and the Wessex and Whirlwind helicopters. By then a Chief Tech, Pat decided to go for a commission in 1985 and went through the RAF College at Cranwell. He was posted to Scampton in February 1986 with the MT Flight, staying there until July 1988 when he came to Waddington and first got to know XH558 during his spare time. This period saw the work up for the complex Sentry, and eventually Pat was made OC A&B at Waddington

Above It gets hot and sticky inside the cockpit of a Vulcan, even on a short trip. Flt Lt Graham O'Connor steps down from XH558. In the background can be seen the more usual movements for Jersey Airport, including a Boeing 737 of Dan-Air – remember them?

Left Following the display at a very appreciative Guernsey, XH558 made a landing back at Jersey around 1210, deploying the braking 'chute and effecting a refuel. In the foreground is Heron 2 G-AORG *Duchess of Britanny* in the colours of Jersey Airlines and operated as a form of 'historic flight' from the island

Above Cpl Taff Stone inspecting some of the stores carried aboard the aircraft during the detachment to Jersey. XH558 shared the ramp at Jersey with Tornado GR.1s of No 27 Sqn. Taff, who worked on XH558's electrics, was stoic about the next posting he would get after VDT and Waddington; he worked with the VDT in the days of XL426 and was then posted to the Red Arrows at Scampton, which eventually included flying with them as a 'back seater' on the way to displays. He joined the VDT again in 1991. Asked what he thought would happen to him after a career in the 'limelight' to date, he said, 'Looks like I may have to join the RAF now!'

Above Such was the occasion that the doors could be put to another use. Huge 'FAREWELL' lettering had been applied down each door, providing spectators with an emotional reminder of what they were witnessing

Right Sgt Terry Kilby, flight systems specialist inspects the plate glazing of the anachronistic bomb aiming blister. The B.2 never had this area equipped, being designed from the start as a 'blind' bomber. VDT said goodbye to Jersey on Friday 18 September with a departure around 1230 hours, heading all the way up the country for Leuchars. The ferry Jetstream took the groundcrew away half an hour later. XH558 touched-down at the Fifeshire Tornado base at 1345 and refuelled. Next day, it displayed at Leuchars then transitted to Finningley for its final RAF show. Over night, preparations were made for its last public appearance. XH558 departed Finningley at 1350 on Sunday 20 September and made its way to Cranfield

XH558 made a wondrous appearance at the Cranfield *Dreamflight* show, flanked by the Hawk T.1s/T.1As of the Red Arrows aerobatic team. This feat had been performed before, at the tenth Great Warbirds Air Display, held at West Malling, Kent, in August 1991. There it had stopped all around in their tracks and at this, the last ever Vulcan show, emotions ran high

Above The Reds peeled away to allow XH558 to undertake its final display alone. The routine, as ever, reflected all aspects of the delta, dwelling not just on its awesome power and the ability to move around the sky with force and dynamism, but also showing its manoeuvrability, and above all, what a beautiful shape and sight it made in the air

Above right XH558 completed its display and touched-down at Cranfield at about 1450 hours to the adulation of the audience, swollen considerably by people there only to see the Vulcan, with the greatest of respect to other performers, such as the Royal Navy and their Lynx HAS.3! The Vulcan was fuelled up and the crew retired to a local hotel for a night of retrospection in the bar!

Right Public following for the Vulcan, especially in its last couple of years as a display aircraft, was – and still is – immense. Following the announcement that the VDT was to stop flying at the end of the 1992 season and be sold off by tender, the response from the public to this decision sent shock waves all around the MoD. Here was an aircraft that united a staggering number of taxpayers and voters

Above In the very year that XH558 faced its pension, the largest supporters organisation of its kind anywhere – the Vulcan Association – collapsed in dismal financial disarray and a bid to breath life into it failed also. Into the gap came a series of determined people who worked hard through the summer months encouraging all and sundry to sign petitions to No 10 Downing Street, to the MoD, to Strike Command and to get people to lobby their Members of Parliament in the hope that the question could be raised in Westminster

Above Even though Parliament was in recess during the last weeks of XH558's final season, the campaigns went on and were never more vociferous than at Cranfield

Above On the morning of Monday 21 September an advance party of the groundcrew left Cranfield and drove home to Waddington in the VDT Sherpa. At about the same time another advance party - of much greater proportions - was assembling all along the A15 road that borders the eastern side of Waddington. The public were going to pay homage one last time. Groundcrew started work on XH558 at Cranfield by 0830 hours and the crew were in at 0900. At 1000, XH558 departed and made a straight in, no frills, approach to a somewhat glum-looking Waddington at 1025. All around, and those in the cockpit, knew that it was just possible that the Avro Type

698 Vulcan had made its last ever flight. It taxied into its dispersal and the mighty engines shut down. The throng of groundcrew and media awaited the flightcrew to emerge

Left It cannot be calculated just how many photos have been taken of XH558. With a backdrop of the B-17G Flying Fortress G-BEDF *Sally B*, a loyal fan takes aim once more on the Vulcan. He is wearing a *Keep the Vulcan Flying* T-shirt, part of the large campaign launched by *Airforces Monthly*

Above Cameras were naturally zooming in on the captain for that flight, Sqn Ldr Paul Millikin. Surrounded by lenses of all descriptions and menacing fluffy microphones, Paul answered what questions he could, but the only one he could not supply was what would happen to XH558. Since that 'last' flight, XH558 has flown regularly from Waddington, so that its aircrew may stay current in order that they may be able to fly the bomber to a new customer. As these words are written no buyer has yet been named for the Vulcan following the MoD's decision to offer it for tender on 1 February 1993. The son of a Lancaster pilot, Sqn Ldr Paul Millikin (he was promoted during 1992) joined the RAF in 1964 and went to No 44 Sqn at Waddington to fly Vulcans after his training. After this, be became a flying instructor at the CFS and then flew Chipmunk T.10s with the Northumberland University Air Squadron. Then came another Vulcan tour, this time as a Qualified Flying Instructor with No 230 OCU at Scampton. It was at this time that Paul became adept at Vulcan display flying. In 1981 came a posting to the Victor K.2 tanker fleet at Marham, during which time Paul flew as a captain on tanker missions in support of *Black Buck* bombing raids. Then he became Chief Flying Instructor with the Victor OCU - No 232 - until its disbandment in April 1986, Paul then moving on to the Training Flight of No 55 Sqn.

During the Gulf War, he completed 30 refuelling missions flying Victors out of Bahrain. Paul was Display Captain with the VDT from 1984 to its disbandment

Above Line-up in front of XH558 as the engines tick as they cool down on the ramp at Waddington on the 'last' day, Monday 21 September 1992. Left to right: Chief Tech Dave Thorpe; Flt Lt Dave Bradford; Flt Lt Al Slack; Sqn Ldr Paul Millikin; Sqn Ldr Dave Thomas; Flt Lt Graham O'Connor; Flt Lt Pat McGeough; and Sqn Ldr Barry Masefield

Technical Specification

Avro Type 698
Vulcan B.2

KEY

1 Wingtip antennae
2 Starboard navigation light
3 Starboard wingtip construction
4 Outboard aileron
5 Inboard aileron
6 Rear spar
7 Outboard wing panel ribs
8 Front spar
9 Leading edge ribs
10 Cranked leading edge
11 Corrugated leading edge inner skin
12 Retractable landing and taxying lamp
13 Fuel tank fire extinguisher bottles
14 Outer wing panel joint rib
15 Honeycomb skin panel
16 Outboard elevator
17 Inboard elevator
18 Elevator hydraulic jacks
19 No 7 starboard fuel tank
20 No 5 starboard fuel tank
21 Diagonal rib

32 Inboard leading edge construction
33 De-icing air supply pipe
34 Fuel collectors and pumps
35 Main undercarriage wheel bay
36 Retracting mechanism
37 Rover airborne auxiliary power unit
38 Electrical equipment bay
39 Starboard engine bays
40 Bristol Olympus Series 301 engines
41 Air system piping
42 Engine bay dividing rib
43 Engine fire extinguishers
44 Jet pipes
45 Fixed trailing edge construction
46 Jet pipe nozzles
47 Rear equipment bay
48 Oxygen bottles
49 Batteries
50 Rudder power control unit
51 Rear electronics bay
52 Electronic countermeasures system equipment
53 Cooling air intake
54 Red Steer tail warning radar scanner
55 Tail radome

64 Fin leading edge
65 Corrugated inner skin
66 Communications aerial
67 Fin de-icing air supply
68 Bomb-bay rear bulkhead
69 Bomb-bay roof arch construction
70 Flush air intake
71 Communications aerial
72 Port Olympus 301 engine
73 Engine bay top panel construction
74 Port jet pipe fairing
75 Electrical equipment bay
76 Chaff dispenser
77 Green Satin navigation radar bay
78 Elevator balance weights and seals
79 Elevator hydraulic jacks
80 Inboard elevator
81 Outboard elevator
82 Inboard aileron
83 Aileron balance weights

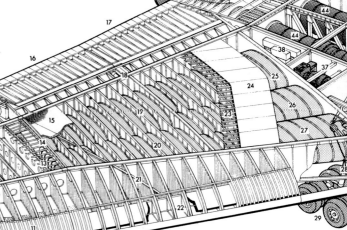

22 Leading edge de-icing air duct
23 Wing stringer construction
24 Parallel chord wing skin panels
25 No 6 starboard fuel tank
26 No 4 starboard fuel tank
27 No 3 starboard fuel tank
28 Main undercarriage leg
29 Eight–wheel bogie
30 Mainwheel well door
31 Fuel tank fire extinguishers

56 Twin brake parachute housing
57 Brake parachute door
58 Rudder construction
59 Rudder balance weights and seals
60 Fin de-icing air outlet
61 Di-electric fintip fairing
62 Passive electronic countermeasures antennae
63 Fin construction

84 Control rods
85 Aileron power control jacks
86 Jack fairings
87 Outboard aileron
88 Port wingtip antennae
89 Retractable landing and taxying lamp
90 Cranked leading edge
91 Fuel tank fire extinguishers
92 Cambered leading edge profile

93 No 7 port fuel tank
94 No 5 port fuel tank
95 Leading edge de-icing air duct
96 No 6 port fuel tank
97 No 4 port fuel tank
98 No 3 port fuel tank
99 Port main undercarriage bay
100 Wing stringer construction
101 Port airbrakes
102 Airbrake drive mechanism
103 Intake ducts
104 Front wing spar attachment joints

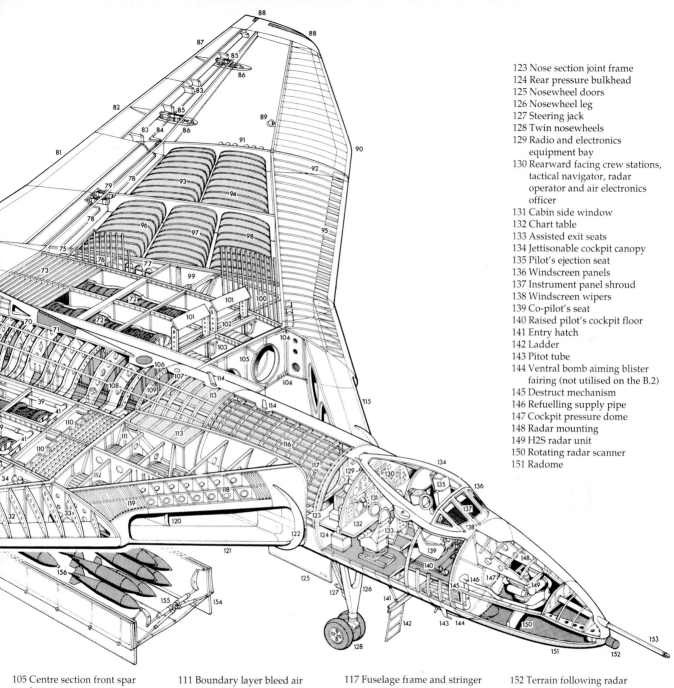

123 Nose section joint frame
124 Rear pressure bulkhead
125 Nosewheel doors
126 Nosewheel leg
127 Steering jack
128 Twin nosewheels
129 Radio and electronics equipment bay
130 Rearward facing crew stations, tactical navigator, radar operator and air electronics officer
131 Cabin side window
132 Chart table
133 Assisted exit seats
134 Jettisonable cockpit canopy
135 Pilot's ejection seat
136 Windscreen panels
137 Instrument panel shroud
138 Windscreen wipers
139 Co-pilot's seat
140 Raised pilot's cockpit floor
141 Entry hatch
142 Ladder
143 Pitot tube
144 Ventral bomb aiming blister fairing (not utilised on the B.2)
145 Destruct mechanism
146 Refuelling supply pipe
147 Cockpit pressure dome
148 Radar mounting
149 H2S radar unit
150 Rotating radar scanner
151 Radome

105 Centre section front spar frame
106 Suppressed aerial
107 Anti-collision light
108 Bomb-bay longerons
109 Forward limit of bomb-bay
110 Starboard airbrake housings

111 Boundary layer bleed air product
112 Starboard intake ducts
113 No 2 fuselage fuel tanks
114 Communications aerials
115 Port engine intake
116 No 1 fuselage fuel tanks

117 Fuselage frame and stringer construction
118 Intake lip construction
119 Corrugated inner skin
120 Intake divider
121 Starboard intake
122 Boundary layer splitter plate

152 Terrain following radar antennae
153 Flight refuelling probe
154 Bomb-bay doors
155 Bomb door opening jacks
156 1000 lb (454 kg) bombs, in three groups of seven

127

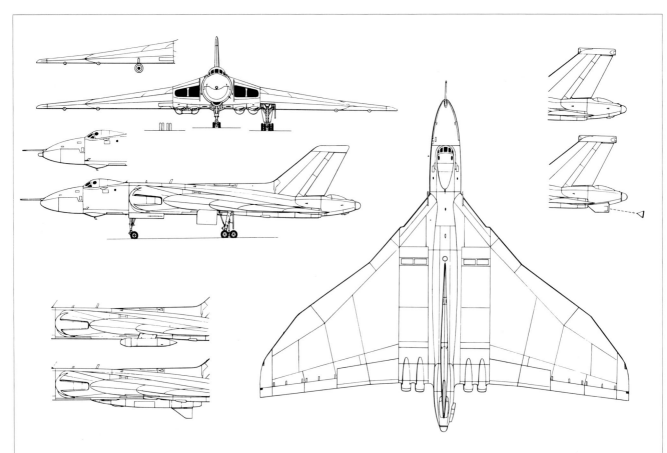

AVRO TYPE 698
VULCAN B.2

Powerplants: Four 20,000 lb Bristol Siddeley Olympus 301 or 17,000 lb st Series 201 turbojets.

Performance: Maximum speed 645 mph (1038 km/h) at 40,000 ft (12,192 m), or Mach 0.98. Maximum cruising speed 627 mph (1010 km/h) at 55,000 ft (16,750 m) or Mach 0.95. Service ceiling 65,000 ft (19,812 m). High altitude tactical radius 2300 miles (3700 km). Tactical radius with low level attack profile 1725 miles (2780 km). In-flight refuelling capability.

Weight: Maximum take-off weight 204,000 lb (92,534 kg)

Dimensions: Wingspan 111 ft 0 in (33.83 m). Length 99 ft 11 in (30.45 m). Height 27 ft 2 in (8.28 m). Wing area 3965 ft^2 (368.3 m^2).

Armament: (Conventional role) Up to 21 1000 lb (454 kg) high explosive bombs internally in bomb-bay. Wing hardpoints capable of accommodating missiles or special mission loads.

Vulcan B.2 production: XH533 to XH539, XH554 to XH563 (17 aircraft); XJ780 to XJ784, XJ823 to XJ825 (8 aircraft); XL317 to XL321, XL359 to XL361, XL384 to XL392,

XL425 to XL427, XL443 to XL446 (24 aircraft); XM569 to XM576, XM594 and XM595, XM597 to XM612, XM645 to XM657 (39 aircraft). XM596 was built, but not fitted-out - it remained at Woodford as a static test specimen. Total production, including XM596: 88 aircraft.

Vulcan B.2 Sqns: Nos IX, 12, 27, 35, 44, 50, 83, 101 and 617 Sqns. Also No 230 OCU (No 27 Sqn flew a number of maritime radar reconnaissance aircraft, designated B.2(MRR), which are occasionally referred to as the SR.2). No 50 Sqn also flew the the six-tanker converted B.2s, which were redesignated K.2s.